Better Homes and Gardens®

ALL-TIME
FAVORITE
Hamburger
& ground
meats recipes

On the cover: Favorite hamburger and ground meat recipes include *Spaghetti Pie* in a pasta crust, *Orange Ham Loaf* topped with orange slices, and *Stir-Fried Beef with Vegetables* over rice. (See index for recipe pages.)

BETTER HOMES AND GARDENS® BOOKS

Editor in Chief: James A. Autry
Editorial Director: Neil Kuehnl
Executive Art Director: William J. Yates

Editor: Gerald M. Knox
Art Director: Ernest Shelton
Associate Art Directors: Randall Yontz,
 Neoma Alt West
Copy and Production Editors: David Kirchner,
 Lamont Olson, David A. Walsh
Assistant Art Director: Harijs Priekulis
Senior Graphic Designer: Faith Berven
Graphic Designers: Linda Ford,
 Sheryl Veenschoten, Tom Wegner

Food Editor: Doris Eby
Senior Associate Food Editor: Sharyl Heiken
Senior Food Editors: Sandra Granseth,
 Elizabeth Woolever
Associate Food Editors: Mary Cunningham,
 Bonnie Lasater, Marcia Stanley, Joy Taylor,
 Pat Teberg
Recipe Development Editor: Marion Viall
Test Kitchen Director: Sharon Golbert
Test Kitchen Home Economists: Jean Brekke,
 Kay Cargill, Marilyn Cornelius,
 Maryellyn Krantz, Marge Steenson

**All-Time Favorite Hamburger and Ground
 Meats Recipes**

Editors: Sandra Granseth, Marcia Stanley,
 Elizabeth Woolever
Copy and Production Editor: Lamont Olson
Graphic Designer: Tom Wegner

Our seal assures you that every recipe in
*All-Time Favorite Hamburger and Ground Meats
Recipes* is endorsed by the Better Homes and
Gardens Test Kitchen. Each recipe is tested
for family appeal, practicality, and deliciousness.

Contents

Ground Meat Tips

Hamburger and other ground meats have been favorites for years. Unquestionably, ground beef is a staple of the American diet.

The term "ground meat" used to mean "hamburger" to most people. And to many it still does. For these people, *Better Homes and Gardens All-Time Favorite Hamburger and Ground Meats* has dozens of recipes and variations for this "all-American" meat. But today, as more and more people search for variety in their diets and bargains at the supermarket, other ground meats are becoming more popular. So, we've also included lots of recipes for ground pork, ham, veal, turkey, chicken, and sausage. And as a bonus, several of the recipes allow you to substitute one meat for another, so you can take advantage of weekly supermarket bargains.

Take time to flip through this book. You'll quickly see that ground meats are adaptable to all kinds of dishes, including casseroles, sandwiches, soups, meatballs, pizzas, sauces, meat loaves, and more. So use your cooking talents and our favorite recipes to make the most of versatile ground meats.

Purchasing Ground Meats:
Ground meats are long-time family favorites and can be bargains in cost per serving. However, knowing the quality of the meat before you buy can help you save money and serve a more satisfying meal.

Federal and state laws regulate ground beef content. It cannot be less than 70 percent lean, and it cannot contain other meats or cereals. Unless otherwise labeled, only skeletal meat—that which is naturally attached to the carcass bones—can be used in making ground beef.

At the meat counter most ground beef products are labeled according to an industry recommendation that all ground meats from the beef carcass be labeled ground beef. The quality distinction between types of ground beef is indicated on the label by the phrase "Not Less Than X% Lean."

Sometimes you will find beef labeled according to the section of the beef carcass from which it was ground. Examples are ground round, ground sirloin, and ground chuck. The quality distinction, however, is not always indicated by the price.

Ground chuck contains the most fat and usually has the lowest price tag of the three. Ground sirloin contains more fat than ground round, but is often more expensive. That's because buyer demand is heavier for meat from the sirloin section.

Occasionally you may find ground meat labeled "hamburger." The amount of fat allowed in hamburger varies according to state laws. The most common difference between hamburger and ground beef is that hamburger can have fat added to it, but ground beef cannot.

For the best value, purchase ground beef with the fat content best suited for your recipes.

1. Use ground beef that is 70 to 75 percent lean when your recipe allows the drippings to be poured off or removed. You can expect this type of ground beef to shrink more than others because of its high fat content.

2. Ground beef that is 75 to 80 percent lean contains enough fat to hold its shape and be juicy, but not so much that it will be greasy. You can expect this type of ground beef to have an average amount of shrinkage.

3. Ground beef that is 80 to 85 percent lean is an excellent choice for low-calorie diets. Unless other ingredients are added to provide moistness, ground beef of this type will not be as juicy as other types.

Neither the government nor the industry has set standard lean-to-fat ratios for ground pork, lamb, veal, ham, or sausage. Sometimes retailers set their own standards and label these meats in a manner similar to the way they label ground beef.

When identifying ground meat, use color as a guide. Ground beef varies from pale red to bright red, ground pork is grayish pink, ground lamb ranges from pinkish red to deep red, and ground veal appears light pink. All brighten when exposed to air.

Storing Ground Meats:
The versatility of ground meats makes them excellent foods to have on hand. But unless wrapped and stored properly, they spoil quickly.

Ground meats spoil more easily than other cuts because more surface area is exposed to air when the meat is ground. Consequently, more of the meat is exposed to micro-organisms that cause spoilage.

If freshly ground meats are prepackaged in plastic wrap or are loosely wrapped, you can refrigerate them safely for one to two days after purchase. Store ground meats in the coldest part of your refrigerator for best results.

Spoilage is indicated by a color change to dull gray, an unpleasant odor, and by the surface becoming sticky or slippery. If there is any indication of spoilage, discard the meat.

Freezing lengthens the storage life of ground meats. Those prepackaged in plastic wrap can be frozen without rewrapping for one to two weeks. However, for longer storage (up to three months), wrap the ground meat in moisture-vaporproof material, seal, and store at 0°F. or below.

Ground meat lends itself to preparation before freezing. Pre-shaping or pre-cooking ground meat can greatly reduce thawing time. Also, pre-shaping can reduce leftovers because you can remove from the freezer the exact number of patties or meatballs to be used in a meal.

Ground raw turkey is being used more often as an entrée at mealtime. It is lower in calories and lower in cholesterol content than most ground meats. Ground raw turkey is most often sold frozen, although you can purchase it fresh. The moisture content varies enough to affect recipes, so if the turkey appears to be soft, decrease the liquid in the recipe by one to two tablespoons.

Bulk pork sausage and bulk Italian sausage are ground from uncured, uncooked meat. Both should be treated as fresh ground meat and stored in the coldest part of your refrigerator. Often you'll find that sausage brands vary in flavor because of the seasoning blends.

Italian sausage differs from bulk pork sausage primarily in the seasoning it contains. Bulk pork sausage usually is seasoned with pepper, nutmeg, and sage. Italian sausage may include fennel, garlic, coriander, nutmeg, paprika, and sometimes red pepper.

Ground veal, ground lamb, and ground pork have their own flavors. But you can expect them to cook similar to ground beef in a recipe. The fat content of veal, lamb, and pork is likely to vary more than that of ground beef because there are no uniform standards.

1 Patties, Loaves, and Meatballs

Use the recipes in this chapter to rediscover favorite ways of serving ground meats in burgers, loaves, and meatballs. This selection of best tasting dishes includes *Meat Loaf Wellington, Spicy Cocktail Meatballs*, and *Burgers Florentine*. (See index for recipe pages.)

2 Soups, Sandwiches, and Pizzas

Add to your list of ground meat favorites from our assortment of soups, sandwiches, and pizzas. On the following pages you'll find hearty main dishes and snacks such as these: *Mexicali Pizza Topping* on *Thin Pizza Crusts, Meal-in-a-Bowl Soup,* and *Russian Fried Pasties.*
(See index for recipe pages.)

Beer-Kraut Heroes

1 beaten egg
1 12-ounce can (1½ cups) beer
¼ cup fine dry bread crumbs
1 pound ground beef
2 tablespoons cooking oil
1 cup thinly sliced onion
2 tablespoons snipped parsley
1 teaspoon instant beef bouillon
    granules
⅛ teaspoon dried thyme, crushed
1 small bay leaf
1 16-ounce can sauerkraut
1 tablespoon cornstarch
6 French-style rolls

In bowl combine egg and ¼ *cup* of the beer; stir in bread crumbs, ¾ teaspoon *salt,* and dash *pepper.* Add ground beef; mix well. Shape into 1¼-inch meatballs. In a heavy skillet brown the meatballs in hot oil; drain off fat. Stir in onion, parsley, beef bouillon granules, thyme, bay leaf, and the remaining beer. Bring to boiling; reduce heat. Cover and simmer about 20 minutes.

Remove meatballs from skillet; cover and keep warm. Discard bay leaf. Drain sauerkraut; rinse if milder flavor is desired. Stir kraut into onion mixture. Bring to boiling. Combine cornstarch and 2 tablespoons *cold water;* stir into sauerkraut mixture. Cook and stir till thickened and bubbly. Split and toast rolls. Place sauerkraut mixture on roll bottoms; top with warm meatballs and roll tops. Makes 6 sandwiches.

Oriental Meatball Salad

2 beaten eggs
½ cup milk
3 cups soft bread crumbs
1 teaspoon onion salt
1 pound ground beef
2 tablespoons cooking oil
1 8¼-ounce can pineapple chunks
2 medium green peppers, cut into
    ½-inch squares
2 medium carrots, sliced
2 stalks celery, sliced
½ cup packed brown sugar
2 tablespoons cornstarch
½ cup dry white wine
⅓ cup vinegar
2 tablespoons soy sauce
2 tomatoes, cut into wedges
    Shredded lettuce

In bowl combine eggs and milk. Stir in bread crumbs, onion salt, and ⅛ teaspoon *pepper.* Add ground beef; mix well. Shape mixture into ¾-inch meatballs. In skillet cook meatballs in hot cooking oil about 10 minutes or till done, turning frequently. Drain off fat.

Drain pineapple, reserving juice. Add water to reserved juice to make ¾ cup liquid. In bowl combine pineapple chunks, green pepper, carrot, celery, and meatballs; set aside. In small saucepan combine brown sugar and cornstarch; stir in the ¾ cup pineapple liquid, wine, vinegar, and soy. Cook and stir till thickened and bubbly. Pour hot mixture over meatball mixture. Cover and chill. To serve, carefully stir tomato wedges into meatball mixture (or, reserve tomato wedges and arrange along edges of plates). Place shredded lettuce on individual plates; spoon meatball mixture atop. Makes 4 servings.

Mexican Meatball Soup

1 medium onion, chopped (½ cup)
1 clove garlic, minced
2 tablespoons cooking oil
2 10½-ounce cans condensed beef
    broth
1 6-ounce can tomato paste
2 medium potatoes, peeled and
    cubed
2 medium carrots, sliced (1 cup)
1 beaten egg
¼ cup long grain rice
¼ cup snipped parsley
½ teaspoon dried oregano,
    crushed
1 pound ground beef

In large saucepan cook onion and garlic in hot oil till onion is tender but not brown. Stir in beef broth, tomato paste, and 4 cups *water.* Bring to boiling; add potatoes and carrots. Simmer for 5 minutes.

Meanwhile, combine egg, *uncooked* rice, parsley, oregano, 1 teaspoon *salt,* and ⅛ teaspoon *pepper.* Add ground beef; mix well. Shape into 1-inch meatballs. Add, a few at a time, to the simmering soup. Return soup to boiling; reduce heat. Simmer about 30 minutes or till meatballs and vegetables are done. Makes 8 to 10 servings.

Meat Patties

Hamburgers

---

1 pound ground beef
4 hamburger buns, split

Seasoning Options: If desired, add any of the following to the ground beef: 2 tablespoons sliced green onion, 2 tablespoons sweet pickle relish, 2 tablespoons chopped pimiento-stuffed olives, 1 tablespoon prepared horseradish, or ¼ teaspoon minced dried garlic.

Shape meat into four ½-inch-thick patties. Panbroil, broil, bake, or grill as directed below. Serve on buns. Serves 4.

To panbroil patties: Heat a heavy skillet till very hot. Sprinkle surface of skillet lightly with salt. Add patties. Cook over medium-high heat till desired doneness, turning once (allow about 6 minutes total time for rare; about 8 minutes for medium; about 10 minutes for well-done). Sprinkle both sides with salt and pepper. If necessary, partially cover skillet to prevent spattering.

To broil patties: Place patties on rack of unheated broiler pan. Broil 3 inches from heat till desired doneness, turning once (allow about 8 minutes total time for rare; about 10 minutes for medium; about 12 minutes for well-done). Sprinkle both sides with salt and pepper.

To bake patties: Place in 8x8x2-inch baking pan. Cover and bake in 350° oven till desired doneness (allow 20 to 25 minutes for rare; 25 to 30 minutes for medium; 30 to 35 minutes for well-done). Sprinkle with salt and pepper.

To grill patties: Mound briquettes in center of firebox. Drizzle with liquid lighter. Wait 1 minute; ignite. Let coals burn for 20 to 30 minutes or till ash-gray. Spread out in single layer. Check temperature of coals (see tip below). Position grill 4 inches above coals; place burgers on grill. (If cooking in covered grill, lower grill hood.) Grill burgers till desired doneness, turning once (see tip below). Sprinkle both sides of burgers with salt and pepper.

Hamburger Grilling Times

Determine the cooking temperature of coals by holding your hand just above the hot coals at the height where the burgers will be cooking. Then count the seconds you can hold that position. If you need to withdraw your hand after 3 seconds, the coals are *medium-hot;* after 4 seconds, the coals are *medium.*

If the burgers cook too quickly because the coals are too hot, raise the grill, close the vents, or remove some hot briquettes. If the burgers cook too slowly because the coals aren't hot enough, lower the grill, open the vents, move coals closer together, or tap ashes from burning coals.

Thickness of Burger	Temperature of Coals	Open Grill		Covered Grill	
		Rare	Medium	Rare	Medium
		(approximate total time in minutes)			
½ inch	Medium-hot	8 to 10	10 to 12	7 to 9	8 to 10
	Medium	10 to 12	12 to 15	8 to 10	10 to 12

  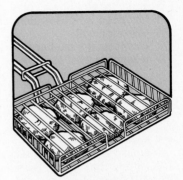

Turn out uniform burgers by starting with equal portions of meat. Just scoop meat into a ½-cup measure, then turn out and shape into a patty. Or, form meat into a roll 4 inches in diameter; cut into ½-inch slices.

Making all of the burgers a uniform size helps ensure that they will cook evenly. Shape burgers carefully, however, because too much handling will give them a compact texture.

For a stuffed burger, spoon desired filling in the center of one patty. Leave a margin of about ½ inch around the edge for sealing to help ensure that the filling stays inside the burger during cooking. Top with a second patty and press the edges of the patties together with fingers to seal. If necessary, gently reshape stuffed burger to make it even.

Using a wire grill basket when grilling burgers makes it much easier to turn them. Choose a hinged basket that allows adjustment to the thickness of the burgers. Open the basket and place the burgers on one side. Hook the other side on top. To turn the burgers, simply invert the grill basket—you don't need to turn them one by one.

Bacon 'n' Cheese Burgers

½ cup chopped onion
2 tablespoons cooking oil
¾ teaspoon salt
   Dash pepper
1½ pounds ground beef *or* ground pork
1 5-ounce jar cheese spread with bacon, softened
2 tablespoons sweet pickle relish
1 teaspoon prepared mustard
6 hamburger buns, split

Cook onion in hot oil till tender but not brown. Combine cooked onion, salt, and pepper. Add ground beef or ground pork; mix well. Shape into six ½-inch-thick patties. Place on rack of unheated broiler pan. Broil 3 inches from heat, turning once. For beef, broil till desired doneness (allow about 10 minutes total time for medium). For pork, broil for 12 to 15 minutes or till well-done.

Combine cheese spread, pickle relish, and mustard. Spread about 1 tablespoon mixture on each bun half. Broil buns about 1 minute or till bun is toasted and cheese is bubbly. Serve patties in buns. Makes 6 servings.

Grilled Sour Cream Burgers

½ cup sour cream dip with French onion
3 tablespoons fine dry bread crumbs
1 pound ground beef *or* ground pork
4 hamburger buns, split, toasted, and buttered

Combine sour cream dip, bread crumbs, ¼ teaspoon *salt,* and dash *pepper.* Add ground beef or pork; mix well. Shape into four ½-inch-thick patties. Grill over *medium* coals, turning once. For beef, grill till desired doneness (allow 12 to 15 minutes total time for medium). For pork, grill about 18 minutes or till well-done. Serve patties in buns. Top with additional sour cream dip, if desired. Makes 4 servings.

Burgers Divan

3 slices bacon
¼ cup chopped onion
1 teaspoon worcestershire sauce
¾ teaspoon salt
½ teaspoon dry mustard
¼ teaspoon dried oregano,
    crushed
1 pound ground beef
¼ cup mayonnaise *or* salad
    dressing
2 teaspoons milk
4 slices tomato
1 small zucchini, thinly sliced
2 tablespoons grated parmesan
    cheese
4 hamburger buns, split and
    toasted, *or* kaiser rolls,
    split and toasted

In skillet cook bacon till crisp; drain, reserving drippings. Crumble bacon. Cook onion in reserved drippings till tender. Combine bacon, cooked onion, worcestershire, salt, mustard, and oregano. Add ground beef; mix well.

Shape into four ½-inch-thick patties. Broil 3 inches from heat till desired doneness, turning once (allow about 10 minutes total time for medium). Combine mayonnaise and milk. Top each burger with 1 tomato slice and a few zucchini slices. Dollop burgers with mayonnaise mixture; sprinkle with parmesan cheese. Broil about 1 minute longer. Serve on buns or rolls. Makes 4 servings.

Beef and Carrot Burgers

1 beaten egg
2 tablespoons milk
½ cup finely shredded carrot
¼ cup finely chopped onion
¼ cup wheat germ
¾ teaspoon salt
¼ teaspoon dried marjoram,
    crushed
⅛ teaspoon pepper
1 pound ground beef
4 slices monterey jack cheese
4 whole wheat hamburger buns,
    split and toasted, *or* kaiser
    rolls, split and toasted
4 lettuce leaves
4 slices tomato

Combine egg and milk; stir in carrot, onion, wheat germ, salt, marjoram, and pepper. Add ground beef; mix well. Shape into four ½-inch-thick patties.

Grill over *medium-hot* coals till desired doneness, turning once (allow 10 to 12 minutes total time for medium). During last minute of cooking time, place a slice of cheese atop each patty. Serve patties on toasted buns or rolls with lettuce and tomato. Makes 4 servings.

Taco Burgers

1 beaten egg
½ cup crushed corn chips
1 1¼-ounce envelope taco
    seasoning mix
1 pound ground beef *or* ground
    pork
1 8-ounce can tomato sauce
4 hamburger buns, split,
    toasted, and buttered
1 large tomato, chopped
1 cup shredded lettuce
½ cup shredded sharp cheddar
    cheese (2 ounces)

Combine egg and ¼ cup *water;* stir in corn chips and *half* of the taco seasoning mix. Add ground beef or pork; mix well. Shape into four ½-inch-thick patties. Grill over *medium* coals, turning once. For beef, grill till desired doneness (allow 12 to 15 minutes total time for medium). For pork, grill about 18 minutes or till well-done. *Or,* place patties on rack of unheated broiler pan. Broil 3 inches from heat, turning once. For beef, broil till desired doneness (allow about 10 minutes total time for medium). For pork, broil for 12 to 15 minutes or till well-done.

Combine tomato sauce and remaining taco seasoning mix. Serve patties on buns. Top with some of the tomato sauce mixture. Pass tomato, lettuce, and cheese. Makes 4 servings.

Well-liked seasonings enhance mayonnaise-topped *Burgers Divan,* stuffed *Oriental Crunch Burgers* (see recipe, page 13), and *Beef and Carrot Burgers* stacked with cheese, lettuce, and tomato.

Swedish Burgers

1 beaten egg
1 cup dairy sour cream
1 cup soft bread crumbs
½ cup finely chopped onion
½ teaspoon dry mustard
½ teaspoon ground mace
1 pound ground beef
½ pound ground pork
8 kaiser rolls, split and toasted
Lettuce leaves

In bowl combine egg and ½ *cup* of the sour cream; stir in bread crumbs, onion, mustard, mace, and 1 teaspoon *salt*. Add ground beef and ground pork; mix well. Shape into eight ½-inch-thick patties. In large skillet brown slowly on both sides. Cover; continue cooking over low heat for 15 minutes.

To serve, place patties on toasted roll halves; spread with the remaining sour cream. Top with lettuce; cover with tops of rolls. Makes 8 servings.

Savory Lamb Burgers

¾ cup soft bread crumbs
⅓ cup milk
¼ cup chopped pimiento-stuffed olives
2 tablespoons finely chopped onion
1 tablespoon snipped parsley
¼ teaspoon dry mustard
1 pound ground lamb
1 tablespoon cooking oil
4 hamburger buns, split, toasted, and buttered

Combine bread crumbs, milk, olives, onion, parsley, mustard, ¼ teaspoon *salt,* and dash *pepper.* Add ground lamb; mix well. Shape into four ½-inch-thick patties.

In skillet cook patties in hot oil over medium-high heat till desired doneness, turning once (allow 10 to 12 minutes total time for medium). Serve on buns. Makes 4 servings.

Bacon Burger Squares

8 slices bacon
2 pounds ground beef
2 tablespoons lemon juice
1 tablespoon worcestershire sauce
8 hamburger buns, split and toasted

Cook bacon till almost done, but not crisp. Cut bacon slices in half crosswise. Pat beef to a 12x6-inch rectangle; cut into 8 squares. Combine lemon juice and worcestershire; brush over patties. Sprinkle with salt and pepper.

Arrange in greased wire grill basket. Place two half-slices of bacon crisscrossed atop each burger. Close basket. Grill burgers over *medium-hot* coals till desired doneness, turning often (allow about 20 minutes total time for medium). Serve on buns. Makes 8 servings.

Beer-Sauced Burgers

2 tablespoons chopped onion
2 tablespoons chopped green pepper
2 tablespoons butter
½ cup catsup
2 teaspoons cornstarch
1 teaspoon worcestershire sauce
½ cup beer
1½ pounds ground beef
6 slices rye bread, toasted

In small saucepan cook onion and green pepper in butter till tender. Combine catsup, cornstarch, and worcestershire; stir into vegetables. Add beer; heat and stir just till boiling. Combine ground beef and 1 teaspoon *salt*. Shape into six ½-inch-thick patties. Brush with beer mixture.

Grill patties over *medium-hot* coals till desired doneness, turning once (allow 10 to 12 minutes total time for medium). Brush occasionally with beer mixture. Serve patties on toasted rye bread; spoon more of the hot beer mixture over patties. Makes 6 servings.

Mushroom-Stuffed Burgers

2 beaten eggs
¼ cup catsup
¾ cup soft bread crumbs
      (1 slice)
¼ cup finely chopped onion
1 teaspoon salt
  Dash pepper
1½ pounds ground beef
1 6-ounce can chopped
      mushrooms, drained
6 slices American cheese
6 hamburger buns, split and
      toasted
6 slices onion
6 slices tomato

In bowl combine eggs and catsup; stir in bread crumbs, onion, salt, and pepper. Add ground beef; mix well. Shape into twelve ¼-inch-thick patties. Place mushrooms atop *half* of the patties to within ½ inch of edge. Top with remaining patties and seal edges.

Grill over *medium* coals till desired doneness, turning once (allow 12 to 15 minutes total time for medium). *Or,* place patties on rack of unheated broiler pan. Broil 3 inches from heat till desired doneness, turning once (allow about 10 minutes total time for medium). Top patties with cheese; heat just till cheese is melted. Serve burgers on buns with onion and tomato slices. Makes 6 servings.

Burgers Florentine (pictured on pages 6 and 7)

1 10-ounce package frozen
      chopped spinach
½ cup small curd cream-style
      cottage cheese (4 ounces)
  Dash salt
1 beaten egg
⅓ cup fine dry bread crumbs
1½ teaspoons salt
2 pounds ground beef *or* ground
      pork
½ of an 8-ounce can (½ cup)
      tomato sauce
¼ cup dry red wine
2 tablespoons chopped green
      pepper
2 tablespoons chopped onion

Cook spinach according to package directions; drain well. Stir in cottage cheese and the dash salt; set aside.

In bowl combine egg, bread crumbs, and the 1½ teaspoons salt. Add ground beef or ground pork; mix well. On waxed paper shape meat mixture into sixteen ¼-inch-thick patties. Place about *2 tablespoons* spinach mixture atop *each* of 8 patties to within ½ inch of edge. Top with remaining patties and seal edges. Place filled meat patties in 13x9x2-inch baking pan. Bake, uncovered, in 375° oven for 30 to 35 minutes. Drain off fat.

Meanwhile, in small saucepan combine tomato sauce, wine, green pepper, and onion. Bring to boiling; reduce heat. Simmer, uncovered, for 8 to 10 minutes. Spoon tomato mixture over burgers. Makes 8 servings.

Oriental Crunch Burgers (pictured on page 11)

1 pound ground beef *or* ground
      pork
¾ teaspoon salt
¼ teaspoon ground ginger
⅓ cup fresh bean sprouts *or*
      canned bean sprouts, drained
¼ cup water chestnuts, drained
      and chopped
2 tablespoons sliced green onion
1 tablespoon soy sauce
4 hamburger buns, split and
      toasted, *or* kaiser rolls,
      split and toasted

In bowl combine ground beef or ground pork, salt, and ginger. Shape into eight ¼-inch-thick patties. Combine bean sprouts, water chestnuts, green onion, and soy sauce; toss together lightly. Place about *2 tablespoons* bean sprout mixture atop *each* of 4 patties to within ½ inch of edge. Top with remaining patties; seal edges.

Place patties on rack of unheated broiler pan. Broil 3 inches from heat, turning once. For beef, broil till desired doneness (allow about 10 minutes total time for medium). For pork, broil for 12 to 15 minutes or till well-done. Serve burgers on buns or rolls. Makes 4 servings.

Cheese-Stuffed Ham Patties

1 beaten egg
⅓ cup milk
½ cup fine dry bread crumbs
½ teaspoon dried oregano,
    crushed
½ teaspoon dried basil, crushed
¼ teaspoon pepper
½ pound ground fully cooked ham
½ pound ground pork
3 slices mozzarella *or* Swiss
    cheese, torn up (3 ounces)
½ cup sliced fresh mushrooms
½ small onion, sliced
2 tablespoons butter *or*
    margarine
½ cup milk
1 tablespoon snipped parsley
1 tablespoon all-purpose flour
½ cup dairy sour cream
2 tablespoons dry sherry

In bowl combine egg and the ⅓ cup milk. Stir in bread crumbs, oregano, basil, and pepper. Add ground ham and ground pork; mix well. Shape into twelve ¼-inch-thick patties. Place cheese atop *half* of the patties to within ½ inch of edge. Top with remaining patties; seal edges. Place in shallow baking pan. Bake in 350° oven for 30 to 35 minutes.

Meanwhile, in saucepan cook mushrooms and onion in butter or margarine till tender but not brown. Stir in the ½ cup milk and parsley. Blend flour into sour cream; stir into mushroom mixture. Cook and stir till thickened and bubbly. Stir in sherry. Season to taste with salt and pepper. Serve over ham patties. Makes 6 servings.

Burrito Burgers

1 8¼-ounce can refried beans
1 4-ounce can green chili
    peppers, rinsed, seeded,
    and chopped
¼ cup chopped onion
1½ pounds ground beef
4 slices American cheese,
    torn up
8 flour tortillas *or* French
    bread slices, toasted
1 cup shredded lettuce
1 medium tomato, chopped

In bowl combine beans, 2 *tablespoons* of the chili peppers, onion, and ¾ teaspoon *salt*. Add ground beef; mix well. Shape into eight ½-inch-thick patties. Place some cheese atop each patty. Fold patty in half; seal edges. Grill over *medium* coals till desired doneness, turning once (allow 12 to 15 minutes total time for medium). *Or,* place patties on rack of unheated broiler pan. Broil 3 inches from heat till desired doneness, turning once (allow about 10 minutes total time for medium).

Heat tortillas on grill or in broiler. Serve burgers in hot tortillas or on French bread with lettuce, tomato, and remaining chili peppers. Makes 8 servings.

Pizza Burger Cups

1 beaten egg
⅔ cup soft bread crumbs
½ cup grated parmesan cheese
⅓ cup finely chopped onion
2 tablespoons snipped parsley
¼ teaspoon salt
⅛ teaspoon garlic powder
1 pound ground beef
1 8-ounce can tomato sauce
1 4-ounce can mushroom stems
    and pieces, drained
¾ teaspoon dried oregano,
    crushed
½ teaspoon fennel seed
1 cup shredded mozzarella cheese

To make meat cups combine egg, bread crumbs, parmesan cheese, onion, parsley, salt, garlic powder, and dash *pepper*. Add ground beef; mix well. On 4 squares of waxed paper pat meat into four 5-inch rounds. Shape each over an inverted 6-ounce custard cup; peel off paper. Place cups in shallow baking pan; refrigerate meat for 1 hour. Bake meat cups, uncovered, in 375° oven about 25 minutes. Allow meat cups to stand about 10 minutes; carefully remove from custard cups. Invert and arrange on baking sheet.

Meanwhile, for sauce combine tomato sauce, mushrooms, oregano, fennel seed, and ¼ teaspoon *salt*. Simmer, uncovered, about 5 minutes, stirring occasionally. Spoon about ⅓ *cup* of the sauce into each meat cup; sprinkle with cheese. Broil 4 inches from heat about 2 minutes or till cheese is melted and lightly browned. Makes 4 servings.

Pita Burgers

2 cups shredded lettuce
1 medium cucumber, seeded and finely chopped
1 8-ounce carton (1 cup) plain yogurt
1 tablespoon sesame seed, toasted
½ cup chopped onion
1 clove garlic, minced
1 teaspoon salt
1 teaspoon dried oregano, crushed
½ teaspoon dried basil, crushed
¼ teaspoon dried rosemary, crushed
1½ pounds ground beef or ground lamb
6 pita bread rounds

Combine lettuce, cucumber, yogurt, and sesame seed; set aside. Combine onion, garlic, salt, oregano, basil, and rosemary. Add ground beef or ground lamb; mix well. Shape into 6 thin patties, each 5 inches in diameter.

Grill over *medium* coals till desired doneness, turning once (allow 10 to 12 minutes total time for medium). *Or,* broil 3 inches from heat till desired doneness, turning once (allow 8 to 10 minutes total time for medium). Split each bread round to make a pocket; place a cooked meat patty inside. Spoon in some lettuce mixture. Makes 6 servings.

Hamburger Steak Diane

1 tablespoon steak sauce
1 teaspoon dry mustard
¾ teaspoon salt
⅛ teaspoon pepper
1 pound ground beef
2 teaspoons butter or margarine
1 3-ounce can sliced mushrooms
1 tablespoon snipped chives
1 tablespoon lemon juice
½ teaspoon worcestershire sauce
2 tablespoons brandy

In bowl combine steak sauce, dry mustard, salt, and pepper. Add ground beef; mix well. Shape into four ½-inch-thick patties. In 10-inch skillet melt butter or margarine. Cook patties in hot butter or margarine over medium-high heat for 3 minutes; turn and cook for 2 to 3 minutes more. Transfer to heated platter; keep warm.

To skillet add *undrained* mushrooms, chives, lemon juice, and worcestershire sauce. Bring to boiling; pour over burgers. Warm brandy in ladle. Ignite; carefully pour over burgers. Serve when flame subsides. Makes 4 servings.

Apricot and Ham Patties

2 beaten eggs
¾ cup milk
1½ cups soft bread crumbs (2 slices)
½ cup finely snipped dried apricots
¼ cup chopped onion
2 tablespoons snipped parsley
Dash pepper
1 pound ground fully cooked ham
1 pound ground pork
⅓ cup packed brown sugar
1 teaspoon all-purpose flour
Snipped parsley (optional)

Combine eggs and milk. Stir in bread crumbs, dried apricots, onion, the 2 tablespoons snipped parsley, and pepper. Add ground ham and ground pork; mix well. Shape meat mixture into eight ½-inch-thick patties. Combine brown sugar and flour; sprinkle in bottom of 15x10x1-inch baking pan. Place patties in pan. Bake in 350° oven for 35 to 40 minutes.

Transfer patties to serving platter. Stir together the pan juices and spoon over meat. Garnish with additional snipped parsley, if desired. Makes 8 servings.

Sauerbraten Burgers

½ cup crushed gingersnaps
    (8 cookies)
1 8-ounce can tomato sauce
¼ cup finely chopped onion
¼ cup raisins (optional)
½ teaspoon salt
1 pound ground beef
2 tablespoons brown sugar
2 tablespoons vinegar
2 tablespoons water
1 teaspoon prepared mustard
    Dash pepper
    Hot cooked noodles *or* rice

Reserve *2 tablespoons* of the crushed gingersnaps. Combine remaining gingersnaps, *2 tablespoons* tomato sauce, onion, raisins, and salt. Add meat; mix well. Shape into four ½-inch-thick patties. Brown in skillet; drain off fat. Combine remaining tomato sauce, sugar, vinegar, water, mustard, and pepper. Pour over burgers. Cover; simmer for 10 to 15 minutes, spooning sauce over meat. Remove burgers.

Stir the reserved 2 tablespoons gingersnaps into sauce in skillet. Cook and stir till bubbly. Return burgers to skillet; heat through. Serve with noodles or rice. Makes 4 servings.

Microwave cooking directions: Prepare patties as above. Place in 8x8x2-inch nonmetal baking dish. Cover with waxed paper. Cook in countertop microwave oven on high power for 3 minutes. Give dish a half-turn; micro-cook 2 minutes more. Drain off fat. Combine reserved gingersnaps, remaining tomato sauce, brown sugar, vinegar, water, mustard, and pepper; pour over burgers. Micro-cook, covered, for 2 minutes. Stir sauce and turn dish; micro-cook, covered, about 2 minutes more. Serve with noodles or rice.

Lamb Patties with Dill Sauce

6 slices bacon
1 beaten egg
¼ cup regular *or* quick-cooking
    rolled oats
¼ cup chopped onion
1 teaspoon salt
    Dash pepper
1½ pounds ground lamb *or* ground
    raw turkey
1 tablespoon chopped onion
1 tablespoon butter *or* margarine
1 tablespoon all-purpose flour
½ teaspoon dried dillweed
½ teaspoon paprika
1 cup milk
2 tablespoons grated parmesan
    cheese

Cook bacon till almost done, but not crisp. Drain; set aside. In bowl combine egg, rolled oats, ¼ cup onion, salt, and pepper. Add ground lamb or ground turkey; mix well. Shape into six 1-inch-thick patties. Wrap a bacon slice around side of each patty; fasten with wooden pick.

Place on rack of unheated broiler pan. Broil 3 inches from heat, turning once. For lamb, broil till desired doneness (allow 12 to 14 minutes total time for medium). For turkey, broil for 14 to 16 minutes or till well-done.

To make sauce, in saucepan cook 1 tablespoon chopped onion in butter or margarine till tender but not brown. Stir in flour, dillweed, paprika, and ⅛ teaspoon *salt*. Add milk all at once. Cook, stirring constantly, till thickened and bubbly; cook and stir 2 minutes more. Stir in parmesan cheese. Remove wooden picks from meat patties. Spoon sauce over patties. Makes 6 servings.

Turkey Burgers

1 beaten egg
½ cup herb-seasoned stuffing mix
1 tablespoon minced dried onion
1 teaspoon instant chicken
    bouillon granules
1 pound ground raw turkey *or*
    ground veal
1 cup herb-seasoned stuffing
    mix, crushed
2 to 3 tablespoons cooking oil
    Cranberry-orange relish

In bowl combine egg and ¼ cup *water*. Stir in ½ cup stuffing mix, dried onion, bouillon granules, and ¼ teaspoon *salt*. Let stand for 5 minutes. Add ground turkey or ground veal; mix well. Shape into five ½-inch-thick patties. Coat with the 1 cup crushed stuffing mix.

Cook patties in hot oil over medium heat about 10 minutes, turning once (turkey burgers should be well-done). Top with a little cranberry-orange relish. Garnish with celery leaves, if desired. Makes 5 servings.

This unusual trio of burgers features sweet yet tangy *Sauerbraten Burgers*, bacon-wrapped *Lamb Patties with Dill Sauce*, and *Turkey Burgers* accented with cranberry-orange relish.

Meat Loaves

Everyday Meat Loaf

  2 **beaten eggs**
  ¾ **cup milk**
  ½ **cup fine dry bread crumbs**
  ¼ **cup finely chopped onion**
  2 **tablespoons snipped parsley**
    (optional)
  1 **teaspoon salt**
  ½ **teaspoon ground sage**
  ⅛ **teaspoon pepper**
1½ **pounds ground beef**
  ¼ **cup catsup**
  2 **tablespoons brown sugar**
  1 **teaspoon dry mustard**

In bowl combine eggs and milk. Stir in bread crumbs, onion, parsley, salt, sage, and pepper. Add ground beef; mix well.

Shape meat mixture into desired shape. For an oblong meat loaf, pat meat mixture into an 8x4x2-inch loaf pan. For a round meat loaf, shape meat mixture into an 8-inch round in a shallow baking pan. For a ring-shaped loaf, pat meat mixture into a 5½-cup ring mold; unmold into a shallow baking pan. For muffin pan meat loaves, pat meat mixture into 18 muffin cups.

Bake meat loaf, uncovered, in a 350° oven (allow 1¼ hours for an oblong loaf; 50 minutes for a round loaf or ring-shaped loaf; 20 minutes for muffin pan loaves). Spoon off excess fat. Combine catsup, brown sugar, and dry mustard; spread over meat loaf. Return to oven; bake about 10 minutes more. Makes 6 servings.

Microwave cooking directions: Prepare meat mixture as directed above. Pat mixture into a 5½-cup ring mold. Unmold into a 9- or 10-inch nonmetal pie plate. (Do not use a loaf pan or muffin pan.) Cover with waxed paper. Cook in a countertop microwave oven on high power for 12 to 13 minutes or till meat is done; give dish a quarter turn every 3 minutes. Spoon off excess fat. Combine catsup, brown sugar, and mustard; spread over meat. Let stand for 5 minutes. Transfer meat loaf to serving platter.

To shape meat into an oblong loaf, turn meat mixture into a loaf pan (a metal pan or glass loaf dish may be used). Slightly press meat down around edges, pulling it away from sides of pan. Smooth top.

Or, turn meat mixture into a large shallow baking pan, such as a 13x9x2-inch baking pan, and shape into an 8x4-inch oblong loaf or an 8-inch round loaf. Smooth top.

To shape meat into a ring-shaped loaf, evenly spoon meat mixture into a ring mold; do not grease the mold. (To check size of mold, fill it with a measured amount of water.) Using your hands or the back of a spoon, firmly pat the meat mixture into the mold so it will hold its shape when unmolded.

Unmold into a shallow baking pan with sides; do not use a baking sheet. Remove mold.

To shape meat into muffin pan loaves, evenly spoon meat mixture into muffin cups. Slightly press meat down around the edge, pulling it away from the side of the muffin cup. Smooth the top of each loaf.

Shaping the meat mixture into small rounds is an unusual way to present a meat loaf. Muffin pan meat loaves also cook much faster than traditional shapes.

Meat Loaf Wellington (pictured on pages 6 and 7)

1 beaten egg
¼ cup dry red wine
¼ cup water
2 cups soft bread crumbs
2 tablespoons finely chopped onion
1 teaspoon salt
1½ pounds ground beef
1 10-ounce package (6) frozen patty shells, thawed
¼ cup canned liver spread
1 beaten egg
   Wine and Olive Sauce
   Cilantro or parsley sprigs (optional)
   Radish rose (optional)

Combine 1 egg, wine, and water. Stir in bread crumbs, onion, and salt. Add meat; mix well. Pat into 8x4x2-inch loaf pan. Bake in 350° oven for 40 minutes. Drain off fat. Remove meat from pan. Increase oven temperature to 400°.

On lightly floured surface press 3 patty shells together; roll to a 10x6-inch rectangle, cutting and patching as needed. Place pastry in shallow baking pan. Carefully transfer meat onto center of pastry. Spread top and sides of meat with liver spread. Press remaining patty shells together; roll to a 10x6-inch rectangle. Place over meat. Brush edges of bottom pastry with some of the remaining beaten egg. Seal top pastry to bottom; trim and reserve edges. Cut decorations from trimmings; arrange atop loaf. Brush pastry with remaining beaten egg. Bake in 400° oven for 30 to 35 minutes. Serve with Wine and Olive Sauce. If desired, garnish with cilantro and radish rose. Serves 6.

Wine and Olive Sauce: Melt 2 tablespoons *butter*. Blend in 4½ teaspoons *cornstarch*. Stir in 1 cup *condensed beef broth;* cook and stir till bubbly. Stir in ¼ cup sliced pitted *ripe olives* and ¼ cup dry *red wine;* simmer for 5 minutes.

Lamb Pinwheel

¾ pound ground lamb
1 2-ounce can chopped mushrooms, drained
2 tablespoons chopped onion
2 tablespoons sweet pickle relish
1 tablespoon snipped parsley
¼ teaspoon salt
   Dash pepper
1½ cups all-purpose flour
1½ teaspoons baking powder
½ teaspoon salt
¼ cup shortening
½ cup milk
   Sour Cream-Dill Sauce

In skillet combine ground lamb, mushrooms, onion, pickle relish, parsley, salt, and pepper. Cover and cook over medium-low heat for 10 minutes, stirring occasionally; drain. Stir together flour, baking powder, and salt. Cut in shortening till mixture resembles coarse cornmeal. Add milk all at once; stir just till blended.

On lightly floured surface knead dough 8 to 10 strokes. Roll to a 10x7-inch rectangle. Spread meat mixture evenly over pastry. Starting at short side, roll up jelly-roll style. Seal seam. Place, seam side down, on lightly greased baking sheet. Brush with a little additional milk, if desired. Bake in 400° oven about 30 minutes. Slice to serve. Pass Sour Cream-Dill Sauce. Makes 4 to 6 servings.

Sour Cream-Dill Sauce: In saucepan stir 1 tablespoon all-purpose *flour,* 1 teaspoon dried *dillweed,* and ¼ teaspoon *salt* into ½ cup dairy *sour cream.* Stir in ½ cup *milk.* Cook and stir over medium heat till thickened and bubbly.

Ham in Cheese Crust

1 cup whole wheat flour
⅔ cup shredded cheddar cheese
⅓ cup cooking oil
2 beaten eggs
½ cup light cream
¼ cup finely chopped onion
¼ cup chopped green pepper
1 tablespoon prepared mustard
1 teaspoon prepared horseradish
1 pound ground fully cooked ham

For crust combine flour and cheese; stir in oil. Reserve ½ cup of the mixture. Press remaining mixture onto bottom and sides of 9-inch pie plate. Bake in 400° oven for 10 minutes. Remove from oven. Reduce oven temperature to 350°.

In bowl combine eggs and light cream. Stir in onion, green pepper, mustard, and horseradish. Add ground ham; mix well. Turn into baked crust. Bake in 350° oven for 35 minutes. Sprinkle reserved crust mixture around edge; bake for 5 minutes more. Let stand for 5 minutes. Garnish with green pepper rings, if desired. Makes 6 servings.

Meat loaves take on a variety of forms, including *Individual Glazed Lamb Loaves* (see recipe, page 25), airy *Meat Loaf Puff,* and *Corn Bread-Topped Ham Loaf* flavored with apricot.

Meat Loaf Puff

1 beaten egg
¾ cup milk
1½ cups soft bread crumbs
    (2 slices)
½ cup chopped onion
1½ teaspoons salt
⅛ teaspoon pepper
1½ pounds ground beef
2 medium tomatoes, peeled and
    sliced
6 slices American cheese
3 egg whites
1 cup dairy sour cream
¾ cup all-purpose flour
½ teaspoon salt
    Dash pepper
3 egg yolks

In large bowl combine 1 beaten egg and milk. Stir in soft bread crumbs, onion, 1½ teaspoons salt, and ⅛ teaspoon pepper. Add ground beef; mix well. Pat meat mixture into an 8x8x2-inch baking dish. Bake in 350° oven for 25 minutes. Drain off excess fat. Arrange tomato slices atop partially baked meat loaf; sprinkle with a little salt and pepper. Cover with American cheese slices.

Beat the egg whites till soft peaks form; set aside. In small mixer bowl combine sour cream, flour, ½ teaspoon salt, and dash pepper. Add egg yolks; beat till smooth. Fold beaten egg whites into yolk mixture. Pour egg mixture over cheese-covered meat. Return to oven; bake about 30 minutes or till golden brown. Let stand 5 minutes before cutting. Makes 8 or 9 servings.

Corn Bread-Topped Ham Loaf

2 beaten eggs
⅔ cup milk
1 cup soft bread crumbs
¼ cup chopped onion
2 pounds ground fully cooked ham
½ cup apricot preserves
1 8-ounce package corn muffin
    mix

In bowl combine beaten eggs and milk. Stir in soft bread crumbs and onion. Add ground ham; mix well. Pat meat mixture into a 12x7½x2-inch baking dish. Bake in 350° oven for 30 minutes. Remove meat loaf from oven; drain off any fat. Spread the apricot preserves over top of ham loaf. Increase the oven temperature to 400°.

Prepare the corn muffin mix according to package directions; pour over the preserves-covered ham loaf. Bake in 400° oven about 20 minutes more or till the corn bread layer is done. Makes 8 servings.

Meat Loaf Potato Roll-Up

2 beaten eggs
1 8-ounce can tomato sauce
½ cup finely crushed saltine
    crackers (14 crackers)
¼ cup finely chopped onion
2 tablespoons chopped green
    pepper
¾ teaspoon salt
1½ pounds ground beef
    Packaged instant mashed
    potatoes (enough for 4
    servings)
2 tablespoons snipped parsley
¼ teaspoon dried thyme, crushed
⅛ teaspoon dried marjoram,
    crushed

In bowl combine eggs and ⅓ cup of the tomato sauce. Stir in cracker crumbs, onion, green pepper, and salt. Add ground beef; mix well. On foil or waxed paper pat meat mixture into a 10-inch square; set aside.

Prepare packaged instant mashed potatoes according to package directions *except omit butter*. Stir parsley, thyme, and marjoram into potatoes. Spoon potato mixture across center of meat. Using foil to lift, fold sides of meat over potatoes; seal seam and ends. Place, seam side down, in shallow baking pan. Bake in 350° oven about 45 minutes. Spoon remaining tomato sauce over loaf. Makes 8 servings.

Meat Loaf Florentine

2 **beaten eggs**
½ **cup milk**
1 **10-ounce package frozen chopped spinach, thawed and well-drained**
1½ **cups soft bread crumbs (2 slices)**
2 **tablespoons soy sauce**
1½ **teaspoons salt**
¼ **teaspoon bottled hot pepper sauce**
2 **pounds ground beef Mushroom Sauce**

Combine eggs and milk. Stir in spinach, bread crumbs, soy sauce, salt, and hot pepper sauce. Add ground beef; mix well. Pat mixture into a 9x5x3-inch loaf pan. Bake in 350° oven about 1½ hours or till done. Serve with Mushroom Sauce. Makes 8 servings.

Mushroom Sauce: In saucepan combine one 3-ounce can chopped *mushrooms,* undrained, and 1 tablespoon all-purpose *flour.* Stir in 1 cup dairy *sour cream* and 2 tablespoons snipped *chives.* Cook, stirring constantly, just till mixture is thickened; *do not boil.*

Crockery cooker directions: Prepare meat mixture as above. Shape into round loaf slightly smaller in diameter than electric slow crockery cooker. Crisscross two 15x2-inch strips of foil (double thickness) across bottom of cooker and extend up sides. Place loaf atop, not touching sides. Cover; cook on high-heat setting for 4 hours. Lift loaf from cooker using foil strips. Serve with Mushroom Sauce.

Pork Loaf with Olives

¼ **cup finely chopped celery**
¼ **cup finely chopped onion**
1 **tablespoon cooking oil**
2 **beaten eggs**
½ **cup milk**
2¼ **cups soft bread crumbs (3 slices)**
⅓ **cup thinly sliced pimiento-stuffed olives**
1 **teaspoon salt**
½ **teaspoon dried oregano, crushed Dash pepper**
1½ **pounds ground pork *or* ground lamb**
¾ **cup shredded cheddar cheese (3 ounces)**

Cook celery and onion in hot oil about 10 minutes or till tender but not brown. In bowl combine eggs and milk. Stir in bread crumbs, olives, salt, oregano, pepper, and celery-onion mixture. Add ground pork or ground lamb; mix well. In a 13x9x2-inch baking pan shape meat mixture into an 8x4-inch loaf. Bake in 350° oven for 1¼ hours. Sprinkle loaf with shredded cheese. Return to oven; bake for 3 to 5 minutes or just till cheese is melted. Makes 8 servings.

Microwave cooking directions: Prepare meat mixture as above. In 9-inch nonmetal pie plate shape mixture into ring about 1-inch high around a small juice glass having a 2-inch diameter. Cover with waxed paper. Cook in countertop microwave oven on high power about 12 minutes or till meat is done; give dish a quarter turn every 3 minutes. Sprinkle loaf with cheese. Micro-cook, uncovered, about 1 minute more or till cheese is melted. Remove juice glass; let meat loaf stand 5 minutes before removing to serving plate.

Apricot-Topped Sausage Loaf

2 **beaten eggs**
½ **cup fine dry bread crumbs**
¼ **cup sliced green onion**
¾ **teaspoon salt**
1 **pound bulk pork sausage**
1 **pound ground veal *or* ground beef**
1 **cup water**
½ **cup snipped dried apricots**
½ **cup packed brown sugar**
⅛ **teaspoon ground cloves**
¼ **cup cold water**
1 **tablespoon cornstarch**

In bowl combine eggs, bread crumbs, green onion, and salt. Add pork sausage and ground veal or ground beef; mix well. In a shallow baking pan shape meat mixture into a 7x4-inch loaf. Bake in 350° oven for 1¼ hours.

Meanwhile, in saucepan combine 1 cup water, apricots, brown sugar, and cloves. Cover and simmer about 20 minutes or till apricots are tender. Combine ¼ cup water and cornstarch; stir into apricot mixture. Cook and stir about 2 minutes or till thickened and bubbly. Serve with meat loaf. Makes 8 to 10 servings.

Stroganoff Meat Loaves for a Crowd

2 beaten eggs
1⅓ cups milk
1 cup quick-cooking rolled oats
¾ cup chopped onion
1 tablespoon worcestershire
   sauce
2¼ teaspoons salt
½ teaspoon pepper
3 pounds ground beef
3 4-ounce cans chopped
   mushrooms, drained
1 cup dairy sour cream

In large bowl combine eggs and milk. Stir in rolled oats, onion, worcestershire, salt, and pepper. Add ground beef; mix well. Pat about *one-fourth* of the meat mixture into *each* of two 8x4x2-inch loaf pans; make a shallow depression lengthwise down centers of loaves.

In small bowl combine chopped mushrooms, sour cream, and ½ teaspoon *salt*. Divide between the meat loaves, spreading half in the depression in each loaf. Cover with the remaining meat mixture, pressing firmly to seal edges.

Bake meat loaves in 350° oven for 1 to 1¼ hours or till done. Let stand 5 to 10 minutes before removing from pans. Makes 2 meat loaves, 6 or 7 servings each.

Orange Ham Loaf (pictured on the cover)

3 beaten eggs
½ cup orange juice
½ cup finely crushed saltine
   crackers (14 crackers)
1 tablespoon prepared mustard
1 pound ground fully cooked ham
1 pound ground pork
½ cup orange marmalade
1 tablespoon prepared mustard
1 orange

In bowl combine eggs and orange juice; stir in cracker crumbs and 1 tablespoon mustard. Add ground ham and ground pork; mix well. In a shallow baking pan shape meat mixture into an 8x4-inch loaf. Bake in 350° oven for 45 minutes or till done.

Meanwhile, in saucepan heat together orange marmalade and the remaining 1 tablespoon mustard. Brush loaf with *half* of the marmalade mixture. Bake for 25 to 30 minutes longer. Cut orange into thin slices; halve slices and arrange atop loaf. Brush with remaining marmalade mixture. Garnish with endive and cherry tomatoes, if desired. Makes 8 servings.

Ham and Rice Loaf

2 beaten eggs
¾ cup milk
1 cup cooked rice
½ cup finely chopped onion
½ teaspoon salt
1 pound ground fully cooked ham
1 pound ground veal
   Paprika
¼ cup milk
1 teaspoon minced dried onion
1 cup dairy sour cream
2 tablespoons prepared mustard

In bowl combine eggs and ¾ cup milk. Stir in cooked rice, chopped onion, salt, and dash *pepper*. Add ground ham and ground veal; mix well. Pat mixture into a 5½-cup ring mold; unmold into a shallow baking pan. Sprinkle with paprika. Bake in 350° oven for 60 to 65 minutes.

Meanwhile, combine ¼ cup milk and the minced dried onion; let stand for 5 minutes. In saucepan combine sour cream, prepared mustard, and dried onion mixture. Heat through over low heat; *do not boil*. Serve with meat loaf. Makes 6 servings.

Quick Wheat Germ Meat Loaves

1 cup shredded carrots
1 cup dairy sour cream
½ cup soft whole wheat bread
   crumbs
⅓ cup wheat germ
1 pound ground beef
1 pound ground pork

In bowl combine shredded carrots, sour cream, bread crumbs, wheat germ, 1½ teaspoons *salt,* and dash *pepper*. Add ground beef and ground pork; mix well.

Pat mixture into 16 muffin cups. *Or,* shape into eight 4x2-inch loaves; place in shallow baking pan. Bake loaves in 350° oven (allow 20 minutes for muffin pan loaves; 35 minutes for small oblong loaves). Makes 8 servings.

Chicken Loaf Supreme

2 **cups chopped fresh mushrooms**
¼ **cup finely chopped green
   pepper**
¼ **cup finely chopped onion**
1 **tablespoon butter *or* margarine**
2 **beaten eggs**
1 **5⅓-ounce can evaporated milk**
1½ **cups soft bread crumbs**
¼ **cup diced pimiento**
¼ **cup snipped parsley**
1 **teaspoon salt**
¼ **teaspoon dried marjoram,
   crushed**
⅛ **teaspoon pepper**
4 **cups coarsely ground *cooked*
   chicken (about 1 pound)**
   Cheese Sauce

In skillet cook mushrooms, green pepper, and onion in butter or margarine till vegetables are tender but not brown. In bowl combine eggs and evaporated milk. Stir in bread crumbs, pimiento, parsley, salt, marjoram, pepper, and mushroom mixture. Add ground cooked chicken; mix well.

Line the bottom of a greased 8x4x2-inch loaf dish with foil; grease the foil. Pat chicken mixture into dish. Bake in 350° oven about 45 minutes or till center of loaf is firm. Invert chicken loaf onto platter; remove foil. Serve with Cheese Sauce. Makes 6 servings.

Cheese Sauce: In heavy saucepan melt 2 tablespoons *butter or margarine.* Stir in 2 tablespoons all-purpose *flour,* ¼ teaspoon *salt,* and dash *pepper.* Add 1¼ cups *milk* all at once. Cook and stir over medium heat till thickened and bubbly. Cook and stir 2 minutes more. Remove from heat. Stir in 1 cup shredded *natural Swiss cheese* till melted.

Veal and Raisin Loaf

2 **beaten eggs**
¾ **cup milk**
1 **cup quick-cooking rolled oats**
1 **cup raisins**
½ **cup finely chopped onion**
½ **teaspoon poultry seasoning**
2 **pounds ground veal *or* ground
   beef**

In bowl combine eggs and milk. Stir in rolled oats, raisins, onion, poultry seasoning, 2½ teaspoons *salt,* and ¼ teaspoon *pepper.* Add ground veal or ground beef; mix well. Pat meat mixture into an 8x4x2-inch loaf pan. Bake in 350° oven about 1½ hours. Let stand for 5 minutes before removing from pan. Makes 8 to 10 servings.

Chutney Lamb Loaf

1 **beaten egg**
¾ **cup soft bread crumbs**
½ **cup finely chopped onion**
½ **cup chopped chutney**
¾ **teaspoon celery salt**
1½ **pounds ground lamb**

In bowl combine egg, bread crumbs, onion, chutney, celery salt, and ¼ teaspoon *pepper.* Add ground lamb; mix well. Pat meat mixture into an 8x4x2-inch loaf pan. Bake in 350° oven about 1 hour. Drain off fat. Serve meat loaf with additional chutney, if desired. Makes 6 servings.

Mini Meat Loaves with Dill Sauce

½ **cup milk**
¼ **cup fine dry bread crumbs**
2 **tablespoons finely chopped
   green onion**
2 **tablespoons snipped parsley**
½ **teaspoon salt**
½ **teaspoon worcestershire sauce**
   Dash pepper
1 **pound ground beef**
1 **4½-ounce can deviled ham**
   Dill Sauce

Combine milk, bread crumbs, green onion, parsley, salt, worcestershire, and pepper. Add ground beef and deviled ham; mix well. Pat meat mixture into two 5x5-inch squares. Cut each in half to form two rectangles. Broil meat 4 inches from heat for 5 minutes; turn and broil about 5 minutes longer. Serve with Dill Sauce. Makes 4 servings.

Dill Sauce: Cook 1 tablespoon chopped *green onion* in 1 tablespoon *butter.* Stir in 4 teaspoons all-purpose *flour,* ½ teaspoon instant *beef bouillon granules,* ½ teaspoon dried *dillweed,* ½ teaspoon *paprika,* and ¼ teaspoon *salt.* Add ½ cup *milk* and ½ cup *water.* Cook and stir till bubbly.

Individual Glazed Lamb Loaves (pictured on page 20)

1 beaten egg
1 cup soft bread crumbs
3 tablespoons finely chopped
    onion
1 teaspoon salt
1 teaspoon finely shredded
    orange peel
¼ teaspoon dried rosemary,
    crushed
⅛ teaspoon pepper
1½ pounds ground lamb
¼ cup honey
2 tablespoons orange juice
    Mint sprigs (optional)

Combine egg, bread crumbs, onion, salt, ½ *teaspoon* orange peel, rosemary, and pepper. Add ground lamb; mix well. Shape into four 4½x2½-inch loaves. Place in shallow baking pan. Bake in 350° oven for 30 minutes. Drain off fat.

Meanwhile, for glaze combine honey, orange juice, and the remaining ½ teaspoon orange peel. Brush *half* of the glaze over meat loaves. Bake about 10 minutes longer. Brush loaves with the remaining glaze. Garnish with mint sprigs, if desired. Makes 4 servings.

Microwave cooking directions: Prepare and shape meat mixture as above. Place in 12x7½x2-inch nonmetal baking dish. Cook, covered with waxed paper, in countertop microwave oven on high power for 10 minutes, giving dish a quarter turn every 3 minutes. Drain off fat.

For glaze combine honey, orange juice, and remaining ½ teaspoon peel. Brush *half* of the glaze over loaves. Microcook, uncovered, 1 to 2 minutes longer or till meat is done. Brush with remaining glaze. Garnish, if desired.

Ham and Apple Mini Loaves

¾ cup finely chopped, peeled
    cooking apple
¼ cup chopped onion
2 tablespoons butter *or*
    margarine
2 beaten eggs
1 8-ounce can tomato sauce
¼ cup apple juice *or* milk
¾ cup finely crushed rich round
    crackers (18 crackers)
1 pound ground fully cooked ham
1 pound ground pork
1 tablespoon brown sugar
1 teaspoon worcestershire sauce

Cook apple and onion in butter or margarine till tender. In bowl combine eggs, ¼ *cup* of the tomato sauce, and apple juice or milk. Stir in cracker crumbs and apple mixture. Add ground ham and ground pork; mix well. Pat mixture into six 4-inch individual fluted tube pans or eight 6-ounce custard cups. Place in a shallow baking pan. Bake in 350° oven for 30 minutes. Carefully loosen loaves and invert into the shallow baking pan; remove fluted pans or custard cups. Bake for 20 minutes more.

In saucepan combine the remaining tomato sauce, brown sugar, and worcestershire sauce; heat through. Serve with meat loaves. Makes 6 servings.

Grilled Pineapple Meat Loaves

1 15½-ounce can crushed
    pineapple (juice pack)
2 beaten eggs
1½ cups soft bread crumbs
2 tablespoons chopped onion
2 tablespoons chopped green
    pepper
½ teaspoon salt
⅛ teaspoon pepper
1½ pounds ground beef
1 tablespoon cornstarch
2 teaspoons prepared mustard
¼ cup catsup
2 tablespoons soy sauce
4 drops bottled hot pepper sauce

Drain crushed pineapple; reserve juice. Add water to juice, if necessary, to make 1 cup; set aside for use in sauce. In bowl combine eggs, bread crumbs, onion, green pepper, salt, pepper, and crushed pineapple. Add ground beef; mix well. Shape into five 4x2-inch loaves. Place meat loaves in wire grill basket. Grill over *medium-hot* coals for 20 minutes. Turn and grill for 20 to 25 minutes more or till done.

Meanwhile, in small saucepan blend together cornstarch and mustard. Stir in reserved pineapple juice, catsup, soy sauce, and hot pepper sauce. Cook over *medium-hot* coals, stirring constantly, till thickened and bubbly. Pass with the meat loaves. Makes 5 servings.

Meatballs

Basic Oven Meatballs

1 beaten egg
¼ cup milk
1 cup soft bread crumbs
   (about 1½ slices)
2 tablespoons chopped onion
¾ teaspoon salt
1 pound ground beef

In bowl combine egg and milk. Stir in bread crumbs, onion, and salt. Add ground beef; mix well. Shape into 1-inch meatballs. Place in shallow baking pan. Bake in 375° oven for 25 to 30 minutes. Use meatballs in preparation of recipes found on page 28. Makes 24 meatballs.

Freeze-Ahead Meatballs

3 beaten eggs
¾ cup milk
3 cups soft bread crumbs
   (4 slices)
½ cup finely chopped onion
2 teaspoons salt
3 pounds ground beef

In large mixing bowl combine eggs and milk. Stir in bread crumbs, onion, and salt. Add ground beef; mix well. Shape into 1-inch meatballs. Place *half* of the meatballs in large shallow baking pan; refrigerate the remaining meatballs. Bake in 375° oven for 25 to 30 minutes. Remove from pan; cool. Repeat with remaining meatballs.

Arrange cooled meatballs in a single layer on a baking sheet so that the edges do not touch. Freeze till meatballs are firm. Using 24 meatballs per package, wrap meatballs in moisture-vaporproof freezer bag or container. Seal and label; return to freezer. Use frozen meatballs in preparation of recipes found on page 28. Makes 72 meatballs.

  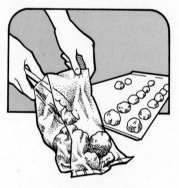

Shaping 1-inch meatballs of uniform size is easily accomplished by gently patting the meat mixture into a 1-inch-thick rectangle on waxed paper. Cut the rectangle into 1-inch cubes. Roll each cube into a ball. You can vary the thickness of the rectangle and the size of the cubes to obtain smaller or larger meatballs.

Another method for shaping uniform-size meatballs is to shape the meat mixture into a roll. The diameter of the roll should be the same size as the diameter that you want for the meatballs. Slice the roll into equal lengths and round into meatballs.

To help prevent ground meat from sticking to your hands, wet your hands with cold water before shaping the meatballs.

When freezing meatballs, arrange cooked and cooled meatballs in a single layer on a baking sheet or in a shallow pan so that the edges do not touch. Place the baking sheet or pan in the freezer. As soon as the meatballs are frozen firm, transfer them to moisture-vaporproof freezer bags or containers and seal. Return to freezer.

Basic Oven Meatballs or *Freeze-Ahead Meatballs* speed the preparation of *Quick Meatball Minestrone* (see recipe, page 28), a hearty soup sure to be enjoyed in chilly weather.

Quick Meatball Minestrone (pictured on page 27)

24 **Freeze-Ahead Meatballs** *or*
   Basic Oven Meatballs
   (see recipes, page 26)
 1 **15-ounce can great northern**
   beans
 1 **tablespoon instant beef**
   bouillon granules
 1 **tablespoon minced dried onion**
 1 **teaspoon dried basil, crushed**
 1 **large bay leaf**
½ **of a 7-ounce package**
   spaghetti, broken into
   2-inch lengths
 1 **16-ounce can tomatoes, cut up**
 1 **16-ounce can mixed vegetables,**
   drained
 1 **teaspoon sugar**
   Grated parmesan cheese

In a 4-quart Dutch oven combine frozen meatballs or Basic Oven Meatballs, *undrained* beans, bouillon granules, onion, basil, bay leaf, and 4 cups *water*. Bring to boiling. Add spaghetti. Cover; simmer about 20 minutes or till meatballs are heated through. Stir in *undrained* tomatoes, mixed vegetables, and sugar. Heat through. Remove bay leaf. Sprinkle individual servings with parmesan cheese. Makes 8 servings.

Meatballs Carbonnade

 3 **slices bacon**
 2 **medium onions, thinly sliced**
 2 **tablespoons all-purpose flour**
 2 **teaspoons instant beef**
   bouillon granules
 2 **teaspoons brown sugar**
 2 **teaspoons vinegar**
½ **teaspoon salt**
½ **teaspoon dried thyme, crushed**
   Dash pepper
 1 **12-ounce can (1½ cups) beer***
24 **Freeze-Ahead Meatballs** *or*
   Basic Oven Meatballs (see
   recipes, page 26)
 2 **tablespoons snipped parsley**
   Hot cooked noodles (optional)

In skillet cook bacon till crisp. Drain bacon, reserving drippings in skillet. Crumble bacon; set aside.

In skillet cook onion in drippings till tender. Stir in flour, bouillon granules, brown sugar, vinegar, salt, thyme, and pepper. Add beer. Cook and stir till mixture is bubbly. Stir in frozen meatballs or Basic Oven Meatballs. Cover; simmer about 20 minutes or till meatballs are heated through. Top with parsley and bacon. Serve over hot cooked noodles, if desired. Makes 4 servings.

Note: For a milder-flavored dish, substitute ¾ cup water for *half* of the beer.

Mexicali Bake

 1 **16-ounce can tomatoes**
½ **teaspoon salt**
½ **teaspoon ground coriander**
 1 **5-ounce jar cheese spread**
24 **Freeze-Ahead Meatballs** *or*
   Basic Oven Meatballs (see
   recipes, page 26)
 1 **16-ounce can hominy, drained**
 2 **to 3 tablespoons canned green**
   chili peppers, rinsed,
   seeded, and chopped
 2 **cups corn chips, coarsely**
   crushed

In blender container combine *undrained* tomatoes, salt, and coriander. Cover; blend till smooth. Add cheese spread. Cover; blend till smooth. Pour into oven-going skillet; add frozen meatballs or Basic Oven Meatballs, hominy, and green chilies. Bring to boiling, stirring occasionally. Transfer to a 350° oven; bake, uncovered, for 30 to 35 minutes. Sprinkle with corn chips. Makes 4 to 6 servings.

Glazed Pork-Bran Balls

1 beaten egg
⅓ cup milk
1 cup raisin bran cereal
1 tablespoon chopped onion
⅛ teaspoon dried thyme, crushed
½ pound ground pork
½ pound ground fully cooked ham
¼ cup packed brown sugar
¼ cup light corn syrup
1 tablespoon vinegar
½ teaspoon dry mustard

In bowl combine egg and milk. Stir in bran cereal, onion, thyme, ⅛ teaspoon *salt*, and ⅛ teaspoon *pepper*. Add ground pork and ground ham; mix well. Shape into 2-inch meatballs. Place in 11x7x1½-inch baking pan. Bake in 350° oven for 30 minutes. Spoon off fat. Meanwhile, in small saucepan combine brown sugar, corn syrup, vinegar, and dry mustard; bring to boiling. Pour over meatballs. Bake about 20 minutes more, basting occasionally with brown sugar mixture. Makes 4 servings.

Porcupine Meatballs

1 beaten egg
1 10¾-ounce can condensed tomato soup
¼ cup long grain rice
2 tablespoons finely chopped onion
1 tablespoon snipped parsley
1 pound ground beef
1 teaspoon worcestershire sauce

Combine egg and ¼ *cup* of the soup. Stir in the *uncooked* rice, onion, parsley, ½ teaspoon *salt*, and ⅛ teaspoon *pepper*. Add ground beef; mix well. Shape into 1-inch meatballs. Place in 10-inch skillet. Combine remaining soup, worcestershire sauce, and ½ cup *water;* add to skillet. Bring to boiling; reduce heat. Cover; simmer 35 to 40 minutes, stirring often. Makes 4 servings.

Greek Meatballs

1 beaten egg
⅓ cup milk
⅓ cup fine dry bread crumbs
⅓ cup snipped parsley
¼ cup finely chopped onion
1 clove garlic, minced
¾ teaspoon salt
¼ teaspoon dried mint, crushed
1 pound ground lamb *or* ground beef
1 tablespoon shortening
Lemon Sauce

In bowl combine egg and milk. Stir in bread crumbs, parsley, onion, garlic, salt, mint, and dash *pepper*. Add ground lamb or ground beef; mix well. Shape into 1-inch meatballs. In large skillet brown meatballs in hot shortening. Cover; cook over low heat for 15 to 20 minutes. Drain off fat. Transfer meatballs to serving dish. Serve with Lemon Sauce. Makes 4 servings.

Lemon Sauce: In saucepan melt 2 tablespoons *butter or margarine;* blend in 2 tablespoons all-purpose *flour,* ¼ teaspoon *salt,* and dash *white pepper.* Add 1 cup *milk.* Cook and stir till thickened and bubbly. Cook and stir 1 to 2 minutes more. Stir in 2 chopped *hard-cooked eggs,* 1 teaspoon finely shredded *lemon peel,* and 2 tablespoons *lemon juice.*

Cherry-Sauced Ham Balls

1 beaten egg
2 tablespoons milk
⅓ cup fine dry bread crumbs
1½ pounds ground fully cooked ham
1 21-ounce can cherry pie filling
1 tablespoon lemon juice
¼ teaspoon ground cinnamon
Dash ground cloves

In bowl combine egg and milk. Stir in bread crumbs and dash *pepper*. Add ground ham; mix well. Shape into 2-inch meatballs. Place in 9x9x2-inch baking pan. Bake, uncovered, in 350° oven for 35 minutes. Drain off any fat. Meanwhile, in saucepan combine pie filling, lemon juice, cinnamon, cloves, and ⅓ cup *water*. Bring to boiling. Pour cherry mixture over ham balls. Return to oven. Bake, uncovered, about 20 minutes. Makes 6 servings.

Meatballs a la Burgundy

1 **beaten egg**
½ **cup milk**
⅓ **cup quick-cooking rolled oats**
¼ **cup finely chopped onion**
1 **pound ground beef**
2 **tablespoons all-purpose flour**
2 **tablespoons burgundy**
1½ **teaspoons instant beef**
    bouillon granules
1 **teaspoon Kitchen Bouquet**
    (optional)
½ **teaspoon sugar**
    Hot cooked noodles

In bowl combine egg and milk. Stir in rolled oats, onion, and ½ teaspoon *salt*. Add ground beef; mix well. Shape into 1-inch meatballs; brown in skillet. Remove meatballs; reserve *1 tablespoon* drippings in skillet. Stir flour into reserved drippings. Add wine, bouillon granules, and 1 cup *water;* cook and stir till thickened and bubbly. Stir in Kitchen Bouquet and sugar; add meatballs. Cover; simmer about 20 minutes. Serve with noodles; garnish with snipped parsley, if desired. Makes 4 to 6 servings.

Beef-Sausage Balls

1 **beaten egg**
½ **cup milk**
½ **cup finely crushed saltine**
    crackers (14 crackers)
3 **tablespoons finely chopped**
    celery
1 **tablespoon snipped parsley**
½ **teaspoon salt**
¼ **teaspoon ground sage**
    Dash pepper
¾ **pound ground beef**
½ **pound bulk pork sausage**
    Parmesan Rice Ring
    Tomato-Onion Sauce

In bowl combine egg and milk. Stir in cracker crumbs, celery, parsley, salt, sage, and pepper. Add ground beef and pork sausage; mix well. Shape into 1-inch meatballs. Place in shallow baking pan. Bake in 375° oven for 25 to 30 minutes. Drain off fat. Place meatballs in center of Parmesan Rice Ring and drizzle with some of the Tomato-Onion Sauce. Pass remaining sauce. Makes 6 to 8 servings.

Parmesan Rice Ring: Combine 3 cups *hot cooked rice* and ¼ cup snipped *parsley*. Press lightly into a greased 5½-cup ring mold. Unmold at once onto oven-proof platter. Combine 1 beaten *egg* and 1 tablespoon *cooking oil;* brush on ring. Combine 3 tablespoons fine dry *bread crumbs* and 3 tablespoons grated *parmesan cheese*. Sprinkle over ring. Bake in 375° oven for 8 to 10 minutes or till golden brown.

Tomato-Onion Sauce: In saucepan cook ¼ cup chopped *onion* in 1 tablespoon *butter* till tender. Stir in one 8-ounce can *tomato sauce*, ¼ cup *water*, 1 teaspoon *worcestershire sauce*, ½ teaspoon *sugar*, and dash *pepper*. Heat through.

Meatballs Stroganoff

2 **beaten eggs**
⅓ **cup milk**
¾ **cup finely crushed saltine**
    crackers (21 crackers)
¼ **teaspoon dried thyme, crushed**
¼ **teaspoon dried oregano,**
    crushed
1 **pound ground beef**
1 **pound ground pork**
2 **teaspoons instant beef**
    bouillon granules
1 **4-ounce can mushroom stems**
    and pieces, drained
¼ **cup all-purpose flour**
1 **cup dairy sour cream**
    Hot cooked noodles

In bowl combine eggs and milk. Stir in cracker crumbs, thyme, oregano, ½ teaspoon *salt,* and dash *pepper*. Add ground beef and ground pork; mix well. Shape meat mixture into 1-inch meatballs. In large skillet brown the meatballs, half at a time; drain off fat. Return meatballs to skillet. Add bouillon granules and 1 cup *water*. Cover; simmer for 20 minutes. Remove meatballs from skillet.

Skim fat from pan juices. Add mushrooms and ¼ teaspoon *salt* to juices in skillet. Combine flour and ½ cup *cold water;* add to juices. Cook and stir till thickened and bubbly. Stir about ½ *cup* of the hot mixture into sour cream; return to skillet. Add meatballs. Heat through over low heat; *do not boil.* Serve with hot cooked noodles. Garnish with snipped parsley, if desired. Makes 8 servings.

Spaghetti and Meatballs

1 beaten egg
¼ cup milk
¾ cup soft bread crumbs
    (1 slice)
⅓ cup grated parmesan cheese
3 tablespoons snipped parsley
¾ teaspoon salt
½ teaspoon dried oregano,
    crushed
    Dash pepper
1 pound ground beef *or* ground
    pork
½ cup chopped onion
1 clove garlic, minced
2 tablespoons cooking oil
1 16-ounce can tomatoes, cut up
2 6-ounce cans tomato paste
½ cup water
1 tablespoon sugar
2 teaspoons dried oregano,
    crushed
1½ teaspoons salt
⅛ teaspoon pepper
1 bay leaf
    Hot cooked spaghetti
    Grated parmesan cheese
    (optional)

In bowl combine egg and milk. Stir in bread crumbs, the ⅓ cup parmesan cheese, snipped parsley, the ¾ teaspoon salt, the ½ teaspoon oregano, and the dash pepper. Add ground beef or ground pork; mix well. Shape into 1-inch meatballs.

In Dutch oven cook meatballs, onion, and garlic in hot cooking oil till meatballs are browned. Drain off fat. Stir in *undrained* tomatoes, tomato paste, water, sugar, the 2 teaspoons oregano, the 1½ teaspoons salt, the ⅛ teaspoon pepper, and bay leaf. Cover; simmer about 30 minutes, stirring occasionally. Remove bay leaf. Serve over hot cooked spaghetti. Pass additional parmesan cheese, if desired. Makes 4 servings.

Meatballs in Chili

1 cup soft bread crumbs
    (about 1½ slices)
⅓ cup milk
¾ teaspoon salt
½ teaspoon chili powder
1 pound ground beef *or* ground
    pork
2 tablespoons shortening
1 16-ounce can tomatoes, cut up
1 15½-ounce can red kidney beans
½ cup chopped onion
½ cup chopped green pepper
¼ cup canned green chili
    peppers, rinsed, seeded, and
    chopped
1 teaspoon dried marjoram,
    crushed
1 teaspoon chili powder
½ teaspoon garlic powder
¼ teaspoon salt
1 bay leaf
1 tablespoon cornstarch
1 tablespoon cold water
    Hot cooked rice

In bowl combine bread crumbs, milk, the ¾ teaspoon salt, and the ½ teaspoon chili powder. Add ground beef or ground pork; mix thoroughly. Shape mixture into 1-inch meatballs. In 12-inch skillet brown meatballs in hot shortening. Drain off fat. Stir in *undrained* tomatoes, *undrained* kidney beans, onion, green pepper, chili peppers, marjoram, the 1 teaspoon chili powder, garlic powder, ¼ teaspoon salt, and bay leaf.

Bring mixture to boiling; reduce heat. Cover and cook over low heat for 20 minutes, stirring occasionally. Remove bay leaf. Combine cornstarch and water; stir into tomato mixture. Cook and stir till thickened and bubbly. Serve over hot cooked rice. Makes 4 to 6 servings.

Spicy Cocktail Meatballs (pictured on pages 6 and 7)

1 beaten egg
¼ cup fine dry bread crumbs
    (1 slice)
1 tablespoon prepared mustard
½ teaspoon salt
⅛ teaspoon pepper
¾ pound ground beef
1 4¾-ounce can liver spread
2 cups corn chips, crushed
1 6-ounce container frozen
    avocado dip, thawed

Combine egg, bread crumbs, mustard, salt, and pepper. Add ground beef and liver spread; mix well. Shape into ¾-inch meatballs. Place in covered container and chill overnight.

Roll meatballs in crushed corn chips. Bake in shallow baking pan in 350° oven about 20 minutes. Serve hot with avocado dip, spearing with cocktail picks. Garnish with fresh hot peppers, if desired. Makes 48 meatballs.

Glazed Sausage Tidbits

1 beaten egg
⅓ cup milk
½ cup finely crushed saltine
    crackers (14 crackers)
½ teaspoon ground sage
1 pound bulk pork sausage
2 tablespoons brown sugar
1 teaspoon cornstarch
¼ cup catsup
1 tablespoon vinegar
1 tablespoon soy sauce

In bowl combine egg and milk. Stir in cracker crumbs and sage. Add sausage; mix well. Shape into ¾-inch meatballs. In skillet brown meatballs slowly on all sides, about 15 minutes. Drain off fat. Combine brown sugar and cornstarch; stir in catsup, vinegar, soy sauce, and ½ cup *cold water.* Pour over meatballs. Cover and simmer for 15 minutes, stirring frequently. Serve hot in chafing dish, spearing with cocktail picks. Makes 48 meatballs.

Mexi-Meatball Fondue

1 beaten egg
¼ cup chili sauce
¾ cup soft bread crumbs
    (1 slice)
½ teaspoon salt
½ teaspoon minced dried onion
⅛ teaspoon garlic powder
¾ pound ground beef
    Cooking oil
    Creamy Avocado Sauce *or* Chili-
    Cheese Sauce

In bowl combine egg and chili sauce; stir in bread crumbs, salt, dried onion, and garlic powder. Add ground beef; mix well. Shape mixture into ¾-inch meatballs.

Pour cooking oil into metal fondue cooker to no more than ½ capacity or to depth of 2 inches. Heat over range to 375°. Add 1 teaspoon *salt.* Transfer to fondue burner. Have meatballs at room temperature in serving bowl. Spear meatball with fondue fork; cook in hot oil for 1 to 2 minutes. Transfer hot meatball to cocktail pick and dip in Creamy Avocado Sauce *or* Chili-Cheese Sauce. Makes 36 meatballs.

Creamy Avocado Sauce: Combine 1 cup mashed *avocado,* ½ cup dairy *sour cream,* 2 teaspoons *lemon juice,* ½ teaspoon *grated onion,* ¼ teaspoon *salt,* and ¼ teaspoon *chili powder;* chill. Stir in 3 slices crisp-cooked and crumbled *bacon.* Thin with a little milk, if desired. Makes 1½ cups.

Chili-Cheese Sauce: Drain one 7½-ounce can *tomatoes,* reserving liquid. Finely cut up tomatoes. Combine tomatoes, 2 cups shredded *American cheese* (8 ounces), ⅓ cup finely chopped canned *green chili peppers,* and ⅓ cup of the reserved tomato liquid. Cook tomato mixture over low heat till cheese is melted, stirring occasionally. Serve warm. (If mixture thickens, stir in a little additional tomato liquid or water.) Makes 1¾ cups.

Filled Lamb Balls

1 tablespoon fine dry bread
   crumbs (¼ slice)
1 teaspoon minced green onion
¼ teaspoon salt
¼ teaspoon curry powder
½ pound ground lamb
2 to 3 ounces *natural* Swiss
   cheese, cut into ½-inch cubes
   Cooking oil

In bowl combine first four ingredients. Add meat; mix well. Shape about *1 teaspoon* meat mixture around each cheese cube to make ¾-inch meatballs. Pour oil into metal fondue cooker to no more than ½ capacity or to depth of 2 inches. Heat over range to 375°; add 1 teaspoon *salt.*

Transfer to fondue burner. Have meatballs at room temperature. Spear meatball with fondue fork; cook in hot oil about 1½ minutes. Transfer to cocktail pick. If desired, dip in plain yogurt. Makes 32 meatballs.

Oriental Appetizer Meatballs

½ cup drained water chestnuts
2 cups soft bread crumbs
½ cup milk
1 tablespoon soy sauce
½ teaspoon garlic salt
¼ teaspoon onion powder
½ pound ground beef
½ pound bulk pork sausage

Finely chop water chestnuts. In bowl combine water chestnuts, bread crumbs, milk, soy sauce, garlic salt, and onion powder. Add ground beef and pork sausage; mix well. Shape mixture into ¾-inch meatballs. Bake in shallow baking pan in 350° oven about 20 minutes. To serve, spear with cocktail picks. Makes 48 meatballs.

Holiday Appetizer Meatballs

2 beaten eggs
⅓ cup fine dry bread crumbs
1 pound ground beef
1 2¼-ounce can deviled ham
1 cup prepared mincemeat
½ cup apple juice *or* apple cider
1 tablespoon vinegar
2 apples, cored and cut into
   chunks

In bowl combine eggs, bread crumbs, ½ teaspoon *salt,* and dash *pepper.* Add ground beef and deviled ham; mix well. Shape mixture into ¾-inch meatballs. Place in shallow baking pan. Bake in 375° oven for 12 to 14 minutes or till done. Cool; remove from pan.

In large saucepan combine mincemeat, apple juice or cider, and vinegar. Heat till bubbly. Add meatballs and apples; heat through. Serve hot in chafing dish, spearing with cocktail picks. Makes 48 meatballs.

Meatball Sandwiches

2 beaten eggs
3 tablespoons milk
½ cup fine dry bread crumbs
1 pound ground beef
½ pound bulk Italian sausage
½ cup chopped onion
½ cup chopped green pepper
1 cup water
1 8-ounce can tomato sauce
1 6-ounce can tomato paste
2 teaspoons sugar
1 teaspoon garlic salt
½ teaspoon dried oregano,
   crushed
¼ teaspoon dried parsley flakes
8 French-style rolls

In bowl combine eggs and milk. Stir in bread crumbs, ¾ teaspoon *salt,* and ⅛ teaspoon *pepper.* Add ground beef; mix well. Shape into 1-inch meatballs. Brown in skillet; remove meatballs. In same skillet cook sausage, onion, and green pepper till sausage is browned. Drain off fat. Stir in water, tomato sauce, tomato paste, sugar, garlic salt, oregano, and parsley flakes. Return meatballs to skillet. Cover; simmer about 15 minutes, stirring occasionally. Cut thin slice from tops of rolls (reserve for another use). Hollow out bottoms, leaving a ¼-inch wall. Fill each roll with 3 meatballs and some of the tomato mixture. Sprinkle with grated parmesan cheese, if desired. Makes 8 servings.

Delight your friends by serving *Oriental Meatball Salad*. Combining meatballs, pineapple chunks, and crisp vegetables, this refreshing salad is sure to be a success. Dieters will like it, too.

Soups

Basic Meat Soup

1 cup dry navy beans
7 cups water
1 10½-ounce can condensed beef broth
2 teaspoons salt
⅛ teaspoon pepper
1 pound ground meat*
1 cup chopped onion
1 clove garlic, minced
1 16-ounce can tomatoes, cut up
2 medium potatoes, peeled and cubed
2 medium carrots, sliced
2 small zucchini, sliced
1 cup vegetables**
½ cup chopped celery
2 tablespoons snipped parsley
1 teaspoon seasoning***
Few drops bottled hot pepper sauce

Rinse navy beans. In 5-quart Dutch oven combine beans, water, condensed beef broth, salt, and pepper. Bring to boiling; reduce heat. Cover and simmer for 2 minutes. Remove from heat. Let stand, covered, for 1 hour. (*Or,* combine beans, water, beef broth, salt, and pepper. Cover and refrigerate overnight.) *Do not drain.* Bring bean mixture to boiling; reduce heat. Cover; simmer for 1½ hours.

In a skillet cook ground meat, onion, and garlic till meat is browned and onion is tender. Drain off fat. Add meat mixture to bean mixture. Stir in *undrained* tomatoes, potatoes, carrots, zucchini, vegetables, celery, parsley, seasoning, and bottled hot pepper sauce. Bring mixture to boiling. Reduce heat; cover and simmer for 30 to 40 minutes or just till vegetables are tender. To serve, ladle soup into individual bowls. Makes 8 to 10 servings.

Meat Suggestions—ground beef, ground pork, ground veal, ground lamb, bulk pork sausage.

**Vegetable Suggestions*—coarsely chopped cabbage, bias-sliced green beans, shelled fresh peas *or* one 10-ounce package frozen peas, peeled and cubed turnip.

***Seasoning Suggestions*—dried thyme, crushed; dried savory, crushed; dried basil, crushed; dried marjoram, crushed; dried rosemary, crushed.

Italian Soup

1 pound ground pork
1 teaspoon fennel seed, crushed
1 teaspoon garlic powder
½ teaspoon chili powder
¼ teaspoon salt
¼ teaspoon pepper
4 slices bacon
2 cups chopped onion
1 teaspoon salt
½ teaspoon garlic salt
6 cups water
3 tablespoons instant beef bouillon granules
1 teaspoon dried oregano, crushed
4 medium potatoes, peeled and chopped (3 cups)
1 10-ounce package frozen chopped spinach

In mixing bowl combine ground pork, crushed fennel seed, garlic powder, chili powder, the ¼ teaspoon salt, and pepper; mix well. Cover and refrigerate meat mixture several hours or overnight to allow flavors to blend.

In Dutch oven cook bacon till crisp; drain, reserving drippings. Crumble bacon and set aside. Cook pork mixture, chopped onion, the 1 teaspoon salt, and garlic salt in reserved bacon drippings for 8 to 10 minutes or till meat is browned and onion is tender. Drain off fat.

Stir in water, beef bouillon granules, and oregano. Bring mixture to boiling; reduce heat. Cover and simmer for 30 minutes. Add chopped potatoes and frozen spinach. Return to boiling; reduce heat. Cover and simmer for 15 to 20 minutes more or till potatoes are tender. Garnish with the crumbled bacon. Makes 8 to 10 servings.

Crockery cooker directions: Prepare and cook pork mixture and bacon as above; drain off fat. Crumble bacon; set aside. In electric slow crockery cooker combine pork mixture, *only 3 cups* water and *half* of the beef bouillon granules, the oregano, and potatoes. Cover and cook on low-heat setting for 8 to 10 hours (or on high-heat setting about 4 hours). Thaw spinach; drain and stir into soup. Turn to high-heat setting; cover and cook about 15 minutes. Garnish with bacon.

Meaty Split Pea Soup

1 pound ground pork *or* bulk pork sausage*
6 cups water
2 cups dry green *or* yellow split peas
2 medium potatoes, peeled and cubed
1 cup chopped onion
½ cup chopped celery
2 teaspoons salt*
1 teaspoon dried marjoram, crushed
¼ teaspoon pepper

In a large saucepan cook ground pork or sausage till browned. Drain, reserving *2 tablespoons* fat in pan. Add water. Rinse split peas; add to meat mixture. Stir in potatoes, onion, celery, salt, marjoram, and pepper. Bring to boiling. Reduce heat; cover and simmer for 45 to 60 minutes or till split peas are tender. Makes 6 to 8 servings.

*Note: If using ground pork, you may want to season the soup with additional salt.

Crockery cooker directions: In skillet brown ground pork or sausage. Drain off fat. Transfer meat to electric slow crockery cooker. Stir in water, peas, potatoes, onion, celery, salt, marjoram, and pepper. Cover and cook on low-heat setting for 10 to 12 hours. Before serving, stir mixture; season to taste with salt and pepper.

Country-Style Bean Soup

2½ cups dry lima beans
8 cups water
1 teaspoon salt
½ pound bulk pork sausage
2 medium apples, peeled, cored, and cubed (2 cups)
2 stalks celery, chopped (1 cup)
1 large onion, chopped (1 cup)
1 clove garlic, minced
1 28-ounce can tomatoes, cut up
2 tablespoons brown sugar
2 tablespoons prepared mustard
1 teaspoon salt
¼ teaspoon pepper

Rinse beans. In 5-quart Dutch oven or kettle combine beans and water. Bring to boiling. Reduce heat; cover and simmer for 2 minutes. Remove from heat. Let stand, covered, for 1 hour. (Or, soak beans in the water overnight in a covered pan.) *Do not drain.* Add 1 teaspoon salt. Bring to boiling. Reduce heat; cover and simmer beans for 1 hour.

In skillet cook sausage, apples, celery, onion, and garlic till sausage is done; drain off fat. Add sausage mixture to beans. Stir in *undrained* tomatoes, brown sugar, mustard, 1 teaspoon salt, and pepper. Bring to boiling; reduce heat. Cover and simmer about 1 hour longer. Makes 8 servings.

Beef-and-Beer Vegetable Soup

1 pound ground beef
1 medium onion, chopped (½ cup)
1 12-ounce can (1½ cups) beer
1 10½-ounce can condensed beef broth
1 soup can (1⅓ cups) water
3 medium carrots, thinly sliced (1½ cups)
1 medium turnip, peeled and chopped (about 1 cup)
1 stalk celery, thinly sliced (½ cup)
1 4-ounce can mushroom stems and pieces
1 bay leaf
1 teaspoon salt
⅛ teaspoon ground allspice
⅛ teaspoon pepper

In large saucepan cook ground beef and onion till meat is browned; drain off fat. Stir in beer, condensed beef broth, water, carrots, turnip, celery, *undrained* mushrooms, bay leaf, salt, allspice, and pepper. Bring to boiling. Reduce heat; cover and simmer for 30 to 35 minutes or till vegetables are tender. Remove bay leaf. Makes 4 to 6 servings.

Crockery cooker directions: In skillet cook ground beef and onion till meat is browned; drain off fat. Transfer meat and onion to electric slow crockery cooker. Stir in beer, condensed beef broth, water, carrots, turnip, celery, *undrained* mushrooms, bay leaf, salt, allspice, and pepper. Cover and cook on low-heat setting for 8 to 10 hours or till vegetables are tender. Remove bay leaf.

Tangy tomato sauce adds zip to *Quick Spanish Hamburger Soup.* Full of ground beef, carrot, and mushrooms, this soup for two makes a satisfying main dish that is easy to prepare.

Meal-in-a-Bowl Soup (pictured on pages 36 and 37)

1 pound ground beef *or* ground
    pork
½ cup chopped onion
3 10½-ounce cans condensed beef
    broth*
1 soup can (1⅓ cups) water*
1 10-ounce package frozen peas
2 large potatoes, peeled and
    cubed
1 cup sliced fresh mushrooms
1 large carrot, chopped
1 small zucchini, sliced (¾ cup)
1½ teaspoons dried basil, crushed
¾ teaspoon ground sage
½ teaspoon salt
⅛ teaspoon pepper

In large saucepan or Dutch oven cook ground beef or ground pork and onion till meat is browned and onion is tender. Drain off fat. Stir in beef broth, water, peas, potatoes, mushrooms, carrot, zucchini, basil, sage, salt, and pepper. Bring to boiling; reduce heat. Cover and simmer about 15 minutes, stirring occasionally. Makes 6 servings.

Note: If desired, substitute 5⅓ cups water and 3 tablespoons instant beef bouillon granules for the condensed beef broth and the 1⅓ cups water.

Spanish Rice Soup

1 pound ground beef *or* ground
    pork
4 cups water
1 28-ounce can tomatoes, cut up
1 cup chopped celery
½ cup long grain rice
¼ cup chopped green pepper
1 1¼-ounce envelope *regular*
    onion soup mix
1 tablespoon instant beef
    bouillon granules
½ teaspoon salt
½ teaspoon dried basil, crushed
    Several dashes bottled hot
    pepper sauce

In large saucepan or Dutch oven cook ground beef or ground pork till browned. Drain off fat. Stir in water, *undrained* tomatoes, celery, *uncooked* rice, green pepper, soup mix, bouillon granules, salt, basil, and hot pepper sauce. Bring to boiling. Reduce heat; cover and simmer about 20 minutes or till rice is tender, stirring occasionally. Makes 6 servings.

Quick Spanish Hamburger Soup

¼ pound ground beef
¼ teaspoon salt
    Dash pepper
1 8-ounce can tomato sauce
1 medium carrot, sliced
1 2-ounce can mushroom stems
    and pieces
2 tablespoons chopped onion
2 tablespoons sliced pimiento-
    stuffed olives
½ teaspoon sugar
½ cup water
¼ cup dry red wine
    Grated parmesan cheese
    (optional)

In saucepan cook ground beef till browned; drain off fat. Stir in salt and pepper. Add tomato sauce, carrot, mushrooms, onion, olives, and sugar. Stir in water and wine. Cover; simmer for 30 to 35 minutes or till carrot is tender, stirring occasionally. Sprinkle individual servings with parmesan cheese, if desired. Makes 2 servings.

Peppy Burger Soup

1 pound ground beef
½ cup chopped onion
½ cup chopped celery
2 cups cubed peeled potatoes
1 16-ounce can tomatoes, cut up
1 10½-ounce can condensed beef
  broth
1 teaspoon sugar
1 teaspoon chili powder
½ teaspoon worcestershire sauce
  Dash cayenne
1 8-ounce can cut green beans

In large saucepan cook ground beef, onion, and celery till meat is browned and vegetables are tender. Drain off fat. Stir in potatoes, *undrained* tomatoes, beef broth, sugar, chili powder, worcestershire sauce, cayenne, 1⅓ cups *water,* and ½ teaspoon *salt.*

Bring mixture to boiling; reduce heat. Cover; cook about 15 minutes or till potatoes are tender. Stir in *undrained* green beans; heat through. Makes 6 servings.

Quick Barbecue Bean Soup

½ pound ground pork
½ cup chopped onion
½ cup chopped celery
1 18-ounce can tomato juice
1 15¾-ounce can barbecue beans
2 tablespoons brown sugar
2 tablespoons prepared mustard
½ teaspoon garlic powder
½ cup shredded American cheese

In large saucepan cook ground pork, onion, and celery till meat is browned and vegetables are tender. Drain off fat. Add tomato juice, barbecue beans, and 1 cup *water.* Combine brown sugar, mustard, and garlic powder; stir into meat mixture. Bring mixture to boiling. Reduce heat; cover and simmer about 10 minutes. Spoon into soup bowls; sprinkle individual servings with cheese. Makes 4 servings.

Sausage Soup

2 slices bacon
1 pound bulk pork sausage
1 medium onion, sliced
1 10½-ounce can condensed beef
  broth
1 8-ounce can *each* French-style
  green beans, cut wax beans,
  and butter beans, drained
½ teaspoon worcestershire sauce
⅛ teaspoon dry mustard

In skillet cook bacon till crisp. Drain off fat. Crumble bacon; set aside. In skillet cook sausage and onion till meat is browned and onion is tender. Remove sausage and onion from skillet; drain on paper toweling. In saucepan combine sausage and onion, broth, green beans, wax beans, butter beans, worcestershire, mustard, 2 cups *water,* ¼ teaspoon *salt,* and dash *pepper.* Heat through, stirring occasionally. Top each serving with bacon. Makes 4 servings.

Quick Cheeseburger Chowder

1 pound ground beef
2 cups cubed peeled potatoes
½ cup chopped celery
¼ cup chopped onion
2 tablespoons chopped green
  pepper
1 tablespoon instant beef
  bouillon granules
2½ cups milk
3 tablespoons all-purpose flour
1 cup shredded cheddar cheese

In large saucepan cook ground beef till browned. Drain off fat. Stir in potatoes, celery, onion, green pepper, bouillon granules, 1½ cups *water,* and ½ teaspoon *salt.* Cover; cook 15 to 20 minutes or till vegetables are tender.

Combine ½ *cup* of the milk and the flour; stir into meat mixture. Add remaining milk. Cook and stir till thickened and bubbly. Add cheese; heat and stir just till cheese melts. Garnish individual servings with additional shredded cheese, if desired. Makes 6 to 8 servings.

Quick Corn-Sausage Chowder

1 **pound bulk pork sausage**
1 **medium onion, thinly sliced**
  and separated into rings
½ **cup chopped green pepper**
2 **17-ounce cans cream-style corn**
1 **12-ounce package frozen loose-**
  pack hash brown potatoes
⅔ **cup milk**
1 **cup shredded American cheese**

In large saucepan cook sausage, onion, and green pepper till meat is browned and vegetables are tender. Drain off fat. Stir in corn, hash brown potatoes, milk, 3 cups *water,* and ½ teaspoon *salt.* Bring to boiling. Reduce heat; cover and simmer about 15 minutes or till potatoes are tender. Add shredded cheese; heat and stir till cheese melts. Serve immediately. Makes 6 to 8 servings.

Beef Chowder

1½ **pounds ground beef *or* ground**
  pork
½ **cup chopped celery**
½ **cup chopped onion**
⅓ **cup chopped green pepper**
1 **28-ounce can tomatoes, cut up**
2 **10¾-ounce cans condensed**
  cream of celery soup
1 **17-ounce can cream-style corn**
½ **teaspoon ground thyme**

In large saucepan or Dutch oven cook ground beef or pork, celery, onion, and green pepper till meat is browned; drain off fat. Stir in *undrained* tomatoes, soup, corn, and thyme. Bring to boiling. Reduce heat. Cover; simmer for 20 to 30 minutes, stirring occasionally. Makes 8 to 10 servings.

Crockery cooker directions: In skillet cook ground meat, celery, onion, and green pepper till meat is browned; drain off fat. Transfer meat mixture to electric slow crockery cooker. Stir in *undrained* tomatoes, soup, corn, and thyme. Cover and cook on low-heat setting for 8 hours.

Beef-Vegetable Stew

1 **pound ground beef**
1 **medium onion, thinly sliced**
  and separated into rings
1 **10¾-ounce can condensed**
  golden mushroom soup
½ **cup French salad dressing**
1 **1-ounce envelope brown gravy**
  mix
2 **tablespoons vinegar**
1 **16-ounce can sliced carrots**
1 **16-ounce can sliced potatoes**
1 **4-ounce can sliced mushrooms**
¾ **cup packaged biscuit mix**
¼ **cup milk**

In 4-quart Dutch oven cook ground beef and onion till meat is browned and onion is tender; drain off fat. Stir in soup, salad dressing, gravy mix, and vinegar. Stir in *undrained* carrots, *undrained* potatoes, and *undrained* mushrooms. Bring to boiling, stirring often. Meanwhile, combine biscuit mix and milk. Drop batter in six mounds atop boiling mixture. Cover; simmer 10 minutes (do not lift cover). Uncover and cook about 10 minutes more. Makes 6 servings.

French Lima Stew

2½ **cups dry lima beans**
1 **pound bulk pork sausage**
1 **cup cubed fully cooked ham**
½ **cup chopped onion**
1 **10¾-ounce can condensed**
  golden mushroom soup
2 **tablespoons catsup**
¼ **teaspoon garlic powder**
1 **bay leaf**

Rinse beans. In 4-quart Dutch oven bring beans and 8 cups *water* to boiling. Cover; simmer 2 minutes. Remove from heat. Let stand, covered, 1 hour. (*Or,* soak beans in water overnight.) *Do not drain.* Simmer, covered, for 1¼ to 1½ hours or just till beans are tender. Drain; reserve *1½ cups* liquid. Cook sausage, ham, and onion till meat is browned; drain off fat. Add meat mixture to beans. Stir in reserved liquid, soup, catsup, garlic powder, and bay leaf. Cover; simmer about 20 minutes. Remove bay leaf. Makes 6 servings.

Spicy Hot Chili

1 **pound ground beef**
1 **medium onion, chopped (½ cup)**
2 **cloves garlic, minced**
1 **16-ounce can tomatoes, cut up**
1 **15½-ounce can red kidney beans, drained**
¾ **cup tomato juice**
1 **4-ounce can green chili peppers, rinsed, seeded, and chopped**
1 **tablespoon worcestershire sauce**
2 **teaspoons paprika**
1 **teaspoon sugar**
1 **teaspoon dried oregano, crushed**
½ **teaspoon ground cumin**
¼ **teaspoon celery salt**
¼ **teaspoon cayenne**
⅛ **teaspoon dry mustard**
  Few drops bottled hot pepper sauce

In large saucepan cook ground beef, onion, and garlic till meat is browned; drain off fat. Stir in *undrained* tomatoes, kidney beans, tomato juice, chili peppers, worcestershire sauce, paprika, sugar, oregano, cumin, celery salt, cayenne, mustard, hot pepper sauce, 1 cup *water,* 1 teaspoon *salt,* and ¼ teaspoon *pepper.* Cover and simmer for 20 to 30 minutes. Makes 4 to 6 servings.

   Crockery cooker directions: (Use a 3½-quart or smaller electric slow crockery cooker because of the small volume of chili.) In skillet cook ground beef, onion, and garlic till meat is browned; drain off fat. Transfer meat mixture to crockery cooker. Stir in *undrained* tomatoes, kidney beans, tomato juice, chili peppers, worcestershire, paprika, sugar, oregano, cumin, celery salt, cayenne, mustard, pepper sauce, *only* ½ *cup water,* 1 teaspoon *salt,* and ¼ teaspoon *pepper.* Cover and cook on low-heat setting for 8 to 10 hours.

Quick Beef and Frank Chili

1 **pound ground beef**
1 **16-ounce package (8 to 10) frankfurters, bias sliced 1 inch thick**
2 **16-ounce cans dark red kidney beans**
2 **15-ounce cans tomato sauce**
1 **28-ounce can tomatoes, cut up**
1 **tablespoon chili powder**
1 **teaspoon dry mustard**
1 **large bay leaf**
1 **cup shredded American cheese**
½ **cup chopped onion**
  Corn chips

In Dutch oven cook ground beef till browned; drain off fat. Stir in frankfurters, *undrained* kidney beans, tomato sauce, *undrained* tomatoes, chili powder, dry mustard, bay leaf, and 1 teaspoon *salt.* Cover and simmer about 30 minutes, stirring occasionally. Remove bay leaf. Serve in bowls; top individual servings with shredded American cheese, chopped onion, and corn chips. Makes 12 servings.

Chili for Two

½ **pound ground beef**
¼ **cup chopped green pepper**
¼ **cup chopped onion**
1 **clove garlic, minced**
1 **8-ounce can tomato sauce**
1 **8-ounce can red kidney beans**
1 **7½-ounce can tomatoes, cut up**
1 **to 1½ teaspoons chili powder**
¼ **teaspoon salt**
¼ **teaspoon dried basil, crushed**
  Hot cooked rice (optional)

In skillet cook ground beef, green pepper, onion, and garlic till meat is browned. Drain off fat. Stir in tomato sauce, *undrained* kidney beans, *undrained* tomatoes, chili powder, salt, basil, and ⅛ teaspoon *pepper.* Bring to boiling; reduce heat. Cover; simmer about 20 minutes. Serve in bowls. Or, spoon over hot cooked rice, if desired. Makes 2 servings.

Chili and Polenta Dumplings

1 pound ground beef *or* ground
   pork
½ pound bulk Italian sausage
½ cup chopped onion
1 28-ounce can tomatoes, cut up
1 15½-ounce can red kidney beans
1 8-ounce can tomato sauce
1 cup chopped green pepper
1 cup thinly sliced celery
2 teaspoons sugar
1½ teaspoons salt
1½ teaspoons chili powder
   Polenta Dumplings

In Dutch oven cook meats and onion till meats are browned; drain off fat. Stir in next 8 ingredients. Cover; simmer for 30 minutes, stirring occasionally. Prepare Polenta Dumplings. Bring meat mixture to boiling; drop dumpling mixture to make 8 mounds atop boiling mixture. Cover; simmer about 12 minutes (do not lift cover). If desired, sprinkle with ½ cup shredded *monterey jack cheese.* Makes 8 servings.

Polenta Dumplings: Combine 1 cup *water,* ⅓ cup yellow *cornmeal,* ½ teaspoon *salt,* and dash *pepper.* Cook and stir till bubbly. Cook 1 minute more. Remove from heat; cool slightly. Add 1 beaten *egg;* beat smooth. Mix ⅔ cup all-purpose *flour* and 1 teaspoon *baking powder;* beat into cornmeal mixture.

Mexican Chili

1 pound ground beef
1 cup chopped onion
2 15½-ounce cans red kidney
   beans
1 28-ounce can tomatoes, cut up
1½ cups chopped celery
1 6-ounce can tomato paste
1 4-ounce can green chili
   peppers, rinsed, seeded, and
   chopped
½ cup chopped green pepper
2 tablespoons sugar
1 bay leaf
1 teaspoon dried marjoram,
   crushed
½ teaspoon garlic powder

In large saucepan or Dutch oven cook ground beef and onion till meat is browned and onion is tender. Drain off fat. Stir in *undrained* kidney beans, *undrained* tomatoes, celery, tomato paste, chili peppers, green pepper, sugar, bay leaf, marjoram, garlic powder, 1 teaspoon *salt,* and dash *pepper.* Bring to boiling; reduce heat. Cover; simmer about 30 minutes, stirring occasionally. Remove bay leaf. Serves 6.

Crockery cooker directions: In skillet cook ground beef and onion till meat is browned; drain off fat. Transfer meat mixture to electric slow crockery cooker. Drain kidney beans; stir in beans, *undrained* tomatoes, celery, tomato paste, chili peppers, green pepper, sugar, bay leaf, marjoram, garlic powder, 1 teaspoon *salt,* and dash *pepper* into meat mixture. Cover; cook on low-heat setting for 8 to 10 hours. Remove bay leaf; stir before serving.

Chili with Limas

5 slices bacon
1 pound bulk pork sausage
1 cup chopped celery
½ cup chopped onion
1 clove garlic, minced
2 10¾-ounce cans condensed
   tomato soup
1 17-ounce can whole kernel corn
1 10-ounce package frozen lima
   beans
1 pickled jalapeño pepper,
   rinsed, seeded, and chopped
   (optional)
1 tablespoon chili powder
1 teaspoon dried oregano,
   crushed
2 cups cubed cheddar *or*
   monterey jack cheese

In large saucepan or Dutch oven cook bacon till crisp; drain, reserving drippings. Crumble bacon; set aside. Cook sausage, celery, onion, and garlic in reserved drippings till meat is browned and vegetables are tender. Drain off fat. Stir in tomato soup, *undrained* corn, lima beans, jalapeño pepper, chili powder, oregano, and 1 teaspoon *salt.* Bring mixture to boiling. Reduce heat; cover and simmer for 20 to 30 minutes, stirring occasionally. Stir in crumbled bacon. Ladle chili into soup bowls. Sprinkle individual servings with cubed cheese. Serve immediately. Makes 6 servings.

Sandwiches

Sloppy Joes

1 pound ground beef
½ cup chopped onion
1 10¾-ounce can condensed
    tomato soup
¼ cup water
1 tablespoon prepared mustard
½ teaspoon salt
¼ teaspoon pepper
6 hamburger buns

In skillet cook ground beef and onion till meat is browned. Drain off fat. Stir in soup, water, mustard, salt, and pepper. Simmer, uncovered, for 2 to 3 minutes. Split and toast buns; serve meat mixture on buns. Makes 6 sandwiches.

Taco Sandwiches

Sloppy Joes mixture (see
    recipe, above)
1 4-ounce can green chili peppers,
    rinsed, seeded, and chopped
1 teaspoon chili powder
1 teaspoon worcestershire sauce
⅛ teaspoon garlic powder
Several dashes bottled hot
    pepper sauce
8 hamburger buns
2 cups shredded lettuce
1 cup shredded American cheese
1 medium tomato, chopped

In skillet combine Sloppy Joes mixture, chili peppers, chili powder, worcestershire sauce, garlic powder, and hot pepper sauce; bring to boiling. Reduce heat; cover and simmer about 5 minutes. Split and toast hamburger buns. Spoon meat mixture onto bottoms of buns; top with lettuce, cheese, tomato, and bun tops. Makes 8 sandwiches.

Beef 'n' Bean Sandwiches

Sloppy Joes mixture (see
    recipe, above)
1 8-ounce can red kidney beans,
    drained
½ cup finely chopped celery
½ teaspoon dried oregano,
    crushed
8 hamburger buns
1 cup shredded cheddar cheese

In skillet combine Sloppy Joes mixture, kidney beans, celery, and oregano; bring to boiling. Reduce heat; simmer, uncovered, about 10 minutes. Split and toast hamburger buns. Spoon meat mixture onto bottoms of buns; top with cheese and bun tops. Makes 8 sandwiches.

Coney Islands

1½ cups Sloppy Joes mixture (see
    recipe, above)
¼ cup chopped green pepper
½ teaspoon chili powder
½ teaspoon paprika
Dash cayenne (optional)
1 16-ounce package frankfurters
8 to 10 frankfurter buns, warmed

In saucepan combine Sloppy Joes mixture, green pepper, chili powder, paprika, and cayenne; heat through. Meanwhile, in saucepan cover frankfurters with cold water; bring to boiling. Simmer for 5 minutes.

To serve, place frankfurters in buns and top *each* with about ¼ *cup* of the meat mixture. If desired, sprinkle with a little shredded cheese. Makes 8 to 10 sandwiches.

Barbecued Pork Sandwiches

1 **pound ground pork**
¾ **cup chopped onion**
2 **cloves garlic, minced**
1 **8-ounce can tomato sauce**
1 **tablespoon vinegar**
2 **teaspoons worcestershire sauce**
¼ **teaspoon fennel seed**
  Few dashes bottled hot pepper sauce
6 **hamburger buns**

In medium skillet cook ground pork, onion, and garlic till meat is browned and onion is tender. Drain off fat. Stir in tomato sauce, vinegar, worcestershire sauce, fennel seed, hot pepper sauce, and ¾ teaspoon *salt*. Simmer, uncovered, for 7 to 8 minutes, stirring once or twice. Split and toast buns; serve meat mixture on buns. Makes 6 sandwiches.

Cheesy Ham Sandwiches

¾ **cup shredded mozzarella *or* cheddar cheese (3 ounces)**
⅓ **cup pizza sauce**
¼ **cup chopped dill pickle**
2 **tablespoons finely chopped onion**
2 **tablespoons chopped green pepper**
½ **pound ground fully cooked ham**
6 **hamburger *or* frankfurter buns**
  Butter *or* margarine, softened

In bowl combine cheese, pizza sauce, dill pickle, onion, and green pepper. Add ground ham; mix well. Split buns; spread with butter or margarine. On bottom of *each* bun spread ⅓ *cup* of the meat mixture; replace top of each bun. Place on baking sheet. Cover with foil. Bake in 350° oven about 20 minutes or till heated through. Makes 6 sandwiches.

Pineapple-Ham Spread

1 **8¼-ounce can crushed pineapple, well drained**
¼ **cup mayonnaise *or* salad dressing**
1 **tablespoon brown sugar**
2 **teaspoons prepared mustard**
½ **pound ground fully cooked ham**
16 **slices rye bread**
  Butter *or* margarine, softened
  Lettuce leaves

In bowl combine pineapple, mayonnaise or salad dressing, brown sugar, and mustard. Add ground ham; mix well. Spread bread with softened butter or margarine. Spread ham mixture on *8* slices of bread; top with lettuce leaves and remaining bread slices. Makes 8 sandwiches.

Chicken Salad Sandwiches

2 **cups ground *cooked* chicken**
½ **cup finely chopped celery**
⅓ **cup chopped sweet pickle**
2 **teaspoons finely chopped onion**
½ **cup mayonnaise**
1 **tablespoon lemon juice**
½ **teaspoon celery salt**
12 **slices whole wheat bread**
  Lettuce leaves
2 **medium tomatoes, sliced**
1 **cup alfalfa sprouts**

In bowl combine ground cooked chicken, celery, sweet pickle, and onion. Combine mayonnaise, lemon juice, celery salt, and dash *pepper;* fold into chicken mixture. Chill.

To assemble, spread bread slices with softened butter or margarine, if desired. Place lettuce leaves on 6 of the bread slices. Top with chicken mixture, tomato slices, alfalfa sprouts, and the remaining bread. Slice each sandwich in half diagonally. Makes 6 sandwiches.

Sandwiches can take unusual shapes, such as *Tacos Con Carne* in taco shells,
Stroganoff Sandwiches on long loaves of French bread, or *Stuffed Pizzas* in pizza crust pastry.

Chow Mein Sandwiches

1 pound ground pork
½ cup chopped onion
1 16-ounce can chop suey
   vegetables, drained
3 tablespoons soy sauce
2 tablespoons cornstarch
8 hamburger buns
½ of a 3-ounce can chow mein
   noodles

In skillet cook ground pork and onion till meat is browned. Drain off fat. Stir in chop suey vegetables. Combine soy sauce, cornstarch, and ⅓ cup cold *water;* stir into meat mixture. Cook about 2 minutes or till thickened and bubbly, stirring to coat vegetables and meat. Split and toast buns; spoon meat mixture onto bottom halves of buns. Crumble chow mein noodles on top of meat mixture; cover with top halves of buns. Makes 8 sandwiches.

Tacos Con Carne

12 taco shells
1 pound bulk pork sausage
1 medium onion, chopped (½ cup)
1 clove garlic, minced
1 teaspoon chili powder
   Shredded lettuce
2 tomatoes, chopped and drained
1 cup shredded cheddar cheese
   Taco sauce

Arrange taco shells on a baking sheet lined with paper toweling. Warm in 250° oven while preparing meat mixture.

In skillet cook sausage, onion, and garlic till meat is browned and onion is tender. Drain off fat. Stir in chili powder and ¾ teaspoon *salt.* Stuff each taco shell with some of the meat mixture, lettuce, tomatoes, and cheddar cheese; pass taco sauce. Makes 12 tacos.

Stroganoff Sandwiches

1 pound ground beef *or* ground
   raw turkey
¼ cup chopped green onion
1 cup dairy sour cream
1 teaspoon worcestershire sauce
⅛ teaspoon garlic powder
1 loaf French bread, unsliced
   Butter *or* margarine, softened
2 tomatoes, sliced
1 green pepper, cut into rings
1 cup shredded American cheese

In skillet cook meat and onion till meat is browned; drain. Stir in sour cream, worcestershire sauce, garlic powder, and ¾ teaspoon *salt.* Heat through; *do not boil.*

Meanwhile, cut bread in half lengthwise. Place halves, cut side up, on baking sheet. Broil 4 to 5 inches from heat for 2 to 3 minutes or till toasted; spread lightly with butter or margarine. Spread the hot meat mixture on toasted bread. Halve tomato slices and green pepper rings; arrange tomato and green pepper alternately atop meat mixture. Broil for 5 minutes. Sprinkle with cheese; broil about 2 minutes longer. Slice to serve. Makes 8 servings.

Stuffed Pizzas

   Pizza Crusts dough (see
      recipe, page 52)
½ pound bulk pork sausage
1 cup chopped onion
½ cup chopped green pepper
2 medium tomatoes, chopped
⅓ cup tomato paste
1 teaspoon dried basil, crushed
½ teaspoon salt
½ teaspoon dried thyme, crushed
1½ cups shredded mozzarella
   cheese (6 ounces)
1 beaten egg

Prepare Pizza Crusts dough as directed. Cover; let rise in warm place till double (about 1 hour). In skillet cook sausage, onion, and green pepper till meat is browned and vegetables are tender. Drain off fat. Combine next 5 ingredients and 3 tablespoons *water;* stir into meat mixture.

Divide dough into 6 pieces. Cover; let rest 10 minutes. On floured surface roll each into an 8-inch circle. Spoon ⅔ *cup* meat mixture onto half of *each* circle; sprinkle *each* with ¼ *cup* cheese. Moisten edge of dough with mixture of egg and 1 teaspoon *water.* Fold in half; seal edge by pressing with fork. Prick tops; brush with remaining egg mixture. Bake on greased baking sheet in 375° oven for 30 to 35 minutes. Makes 6 stuffed pizzas.

Tostadas

1   **pound ground beef**
½ **cup chopped onion**
1   **clove garlic, minced**
¼ **cup taco sauce**
1   **8-ounce can red kidney beans**
2   **tablespoons chopped canned green chili peppers**
    Cooking oil
6   **6-inch flour tortillas**
1   **large tomato, chopped**
2   **cups shredded lettuce**
1   **cup shredded American cheese**
    Creamy French salad dressing *or* taco sauce
1   **avocado, seeded, peeled, and chopped (optional)**

In skillet cook ground beef, onion, and garlic till meat is browned and onion is tender. Drain off fat. Stir in ¼ cup taco sauce and ½ teaspoon *salt*. Set aside and keep warm. In saucepan combine *undrained* kidney beans and chili peppers. Heat through; drain. Set aside and keep warm. In heavy skillet heat ¼ *inch* cooking oil. Fry tortillas, one at a time, in hot oil for 20 to 40 seconds on each side or till crisp and golden. Drain on paper toweling. Keep warm in foil in 250° oven while frying remaining tortillas.

Place tortillas in center of dinner plates. Spoon ingredients over tortillas in the following order: meat mixture, bean-chili pepper mixture, tomato, lettuce, cheese. Serve at once. Pass salad dressing or additional taco sauce. If desired, sprinkle with avocado. Makes 6 servings.

Pork and Liver Pâté Sandwiches

2   **slices bacon, halved**
½ **cup chopped onion**
2   **cloves garlic, minced**
1   **pound ground pork**
4   **ounces chicken livers**
1   **cup milk**
2   **eggs**
2   **tablespoons fine dry bread crumbs**
2   **tablespoons anchovy paste**
1   **tablespoon cornstarch**
2   **teaspoons prepared mustard**
½ **teaspoon dried sage, crushed**
½ **teaspoon dried basil, crushed**
¼ **teaspoon salt**
⅛ **teaspoon pepper**
12 **lettuce leaves**
12 **slices rye bread**

In skillet cook bacon till crisp. Drain, reserving *2 tablespoons* drippings. Set bacon aside. Cook onion and garlic in reserved drippings till onion is tender; add ground pork and chicken livers. Cook and stir over medium-high heat about 5 minutes or till livers no longer are pink. Drain well; cool.

In blender container place ½ *cup* of the milk, pork-onion mixture, and bacon. Cover; blend on medium speed till smooth. Add eggs, bread crumbs, anchovy paste, cornstarch, mustard, sage, basil, salt, and pepper. Cover; blend well. Pour into an 8x4x2-inch loaf pan. Set in shallow baking pan; pour hot water around loaf pan to depth of ½ inch. Bake in 325° oven for 1 hour. Cool; cover and chill. To assemble open-face sandwiches, place lettuce leaves on bread slices; unmold pâté and spread atop lettuce-lined bread. Makes 12 open-face sandwiches.

Note: To use pâté as an appetizer rather than open-face sandwich, unmold pâté and spread on crisp crackers instead of lettuce-lined rye bread.

Ravioli Roulade

1   **10-ounce package frozen chopped spinach**
½ **pound ground beef *or* 6 ounces ground fully cooked ham**
⅓ **cup shredded monterey jack cheese**
1   **package (8) refrigerated crescent rolls**
1   **tablespoon milk**
½ **of a 15½-ounce can meatless spaghetti sauce**
8   **pimiento-stuffed olives (optional)**

Cook spinach according to package directions; drain well. In skillet brown ground beef; season with a little salt. (If using ground ham, do not brown or season the meat.) Combine beef or ham, spinach, and cheese; mix well.

To make sandwiches, unroll crescent rolls; separate into eight triangles. At the wide end of *each* triangle place about ¼ *cup* of the meat mixture. Roll up, starting at the wide end. Arrange sandwiches, point side down, on greased baking sheet. Brush sandwiches with milk. Bake in 375° oven for 20 to 25 minutes or till golden brown.

Meanwhile, heat spaghetti sauce. Serve over sandwiches. Garnish with olives, if desired. Makes 8 sandwiches.

Russian Fried Pasties (pictured on pages 36 and 37)

2½ to 3 cups all-purpose flour
  1 package active dry yeast
  1 cup milk
  1 teaspoon salt
  ¼ teaspoon sugar
  ½ pound ground beef *or* ground
     pork
  ½ cup chopped onion
  1 clove garlic, minced
  ½ cup tomato sauce
  2 tablespoons grated parmesan
     cheese
  2 tablespoons snipped parsley
  ¼ teaspoon salt
  ¼ teaspoon ground cinnamon
  ⅛ teaspoon pepper
  ⅛ teaspoon ground ginger
  3 tablespoons cooking oil

In mixer bowl combine *1 ½ cups* of the flour and the yeast. In saucepan heat milk, 1 teaspoon salt, and sugar just till warm (115° to 120°), stirring constantly. Add to flour mixture in mixer bowl. Beat at low speed of electric mixer for ½ minute, scraping sides of bowl constantly. Beat 3 minutes at high speed. Stir in as much of the remaining flour as you can mix in with a spoon. Turn out onto lightly floured surface. Knead in enough remaining flour to make a moderately stiff dough that is smooth and elastic (6 to 8 minutes total). Place in lightly greased bowl, turning once to grease surface. Cover; let dough rise in warm place till double (about 1 hour).

Meanwhile, in skillet cook ground beef or ground pork, onion, and garlic till meat is browned and onion is tender. Drain off fat. Stir in tomato sauce, cheese, parsley, ¼ teaspoon salt, cinnamon, pepper, and ginger. Heat through.

Punch dough down; turn out onto lightly floured surface. Shape into 12 balls. Cover; let rest 5 to 10 minutes. To make pasties, place each ball of dough on a lightly floured surface. Roll to a 5-inch round as described below. Place about 2 *tablespoons* of the meat mixture atop *each* round. Shape the pasty as described in tip box below.

In heavy 12-inch skillet heat cooking oil over medium heat about 1 minute or till hot. Place 6 of the pasties, seam side down, in the hot oil. Reduce heat to medium-low. Cover and cook for 8 to 10 minutes or till crisp and lightly browned. Turn pasties; cover and cook for 8 to 10 minutes more or till crisp and lightly browned. Remove pasties from skillet. Drain on paper toweling. Keep warm while cooking remaining pasties. (Add additional oil to skillet, if needed.) Serve warm. Makes 12.

Wrapping Russian Pasties

To shape Russian pasties, place each ball of dough on a lightly floured surface. Roll from center to edges to a 5-inch round, rolling thinner at the edges. Place about 2 tablespoons of the meat mixture in center of each round. Moisten edges of dough with a little water. Bring edges of dough up around meat mixture, easing the fullness of the pasty edges into tiny pleats in the center of the pasty. Slightly stretch the pasty edges until they just meet. Pinch the edges together to seal.

Pizzas

Pizza Crusts

2½ to 3 cups all-purpose flour
1 package active dry yeast
1 teaspoon salt
1 cup warm water (115° to 120°)
2 tablespoons cooking oil

In mixer bowl combine *1¼ cups* of the flour, the yeast, and salt. Stir in warm water and oil. Beat at low speed of electric mixer for ½ minute, scraping bowl constantly. Beat 3 minutes at high speed. Stir in as much of remaining flour as you can mix in with a spoon. Turn out onto lightly floured surface. Knead in enough remaining flour to make a moderately stiff dough that is smooth and elastic (6 to 8 minutes total).

Thin pizza crusts: Cover dough and let rest 10 minutes. For 12-inch pizzas, divide dough in half. On lightly floured surface roll each half into a 13-inch circle. (Or, for 10-inch pizzas, divide dough into thirds; roll each third into an 11-inch circle.) Transfer circles of dough to greased 12-inch pizza pans or baking sheets. Build up edges slightly. Bake in 425° oven about 12 minutes or till lightly browned. Add desired pizza topping (see following recipes). Return to 425° oven; bake for 10 to 15 minutes longer or till bubbly. Makes two 12-inch or three 10-inch thin-crust pizzas.

Pan pizza crusts: Cover dough and let rise in warm place till double (about 1 hour). Punch down. Divide in half. Cover; let rest 10 minutes. With greased fingers pat dough onto bottom and halfway up sides of two greased 11x7x1½-inch or 9x9x2-inch baking pans. Cover; let rise till nearly double (30 to 45 minutes). Bake in 375° oven for 20 to 25 minutes or till lightly browned. Add desired pizza topping (see following recipes). Return to 375° oven; bake for 20 to 25 minutes longer or till bubbly. Let stand 5 minutes before serving. Makes two 11x7-inch or 9x9-inch pan pizzas.

Two-crust pizza crusts: Cover dough and let rest 10 minutes. Divide dough in half. On lightly floured surface roll each half into a 13-inch circle. Transfer one circle to greased 12-inch pizza pan or baking sheet. Spread desired pizza topping over dough (see following recipes). Moisten edge of dough with a little water; top with second circle of dough. Crimp edge of dough to seal. Brush top with a little milk, if desired. Prick top in several places. Bake in 375° oven for 45 to 50 minutes. Let stand 5 minutes before serving. Makes one 12-inch two-crust pizza.

Ground Lamb Pizza Topping

1 pound ground lamb
½ cup chopped onion
2 8-ounce cans tomato sauce with cheese
1 teaspoon chili powder
1 teaspoon dried oregano, crushed
½ teaspoon dried basil, crushed
⅛ teaspoon pepper
2 cups shredded mozzarella cheese (8 ounces)

In skillet cook ground lamb and onion till meat is browned. Drain off fat. Stir in tomato sauce, chili powder, oregano, basil, and pepper. Cover and simmer about 10 minutes. Spread desired pizza crusts with meat mixture (see recipe, above); top with shredded mozzarella cheese. Bake as directed in crust recipes.

Beef and Mushroom Pizza Topping

1 **pound ground beef**
1 **15-ounce can tomato sauce**
1 **4-ounce can mushroom stems and pieces, drained**
1½ **teaspoons dried oregano, crushed**
¾ **teaspoon salt**
1 **green pepper, thinly sliced**
2 **cups shredded mozzarella cheese (8 ounces)**

In skillet cook ground beef till meat is browned; drain off fat. Stir in tomato sauce, mushroom stems and pieces, oregano, and salt. Cover; simmer about 10 minutes. Spread desired pizza crusts with meat mixture (see recipe, opposite); top with green pepper slices and mozzarella cheese. Bake as directed in crust recipe.

Italian Pizza Topping

1 **pound bulk Italian sausage**
½ **cup chopped onion**
1 **15-ounce can tomato sauce**
¾ **teaspoon dried basil, crushed**
¾ **teaspoon dried oregano, crushed**
½ **teaspoon salt**
2 **cups shredded provolone *or* mozzarella cheese (8 ounces)**

In skillet cook sausage and onion till meat is browned; drain off fat. Stir in tomato sauce, basil, oregano, and salt. Cover; simmer about 10 minutes. Spread desired pizza crusts with meat mixture (see recipe, opposite); top with shredded cheese. Bake as directed in crust recipe. Sprinkle with ⅓ cup snipped parsley, if desired.

Mexicali Pizza Topping (pictured on pages 36 and 37)

1 **pound bulk pork sausage *or* bulk Italian sausage**
½ **cup chopped onion**
1 **15-ounce can tomato sauce**
1 **cup sliced pitted ripe olives**
1 **4-ounce can green chili peppers, rinsed, seeded, and chopped**
1 **teaspoon dried parsley flakes**
2 **cups shredded cheddar cheese**
2 **tomatoes, sliced (optional)**
Shredded lettuce (optional)

In skillet cook sausage and onion till meat is browned; drain off fat. Stir in tomato sauce, olives, chili peppers, and parsley. Cover; simmer about 10 minutes. Spread desired pizza crusts with meat mixture (see recipe, opposite); top with cheese. Bake as directed in crust recipe. Top with tomato slices and shredded lettuce, if desired.

Ham and Swiss Pizza Topping

1 **beaten egg**
1¼ **cups shredded Swiss *or* mozzarella cheese (5 ounces)**
1 **cup ricotta *or* cream-style cottage cheese, drained**
1 **2-ounce jar chopped pimiento, drained**
2 **tablespoons snipped parsley**
¾ **pound ground fully cooked ham**
2 **tablespoons fine dry bread crumbs**

In bowl combine egg, Swiss or mozzarella cheese, ricotta or cottage cheese, pimiento, and parsley. Add ground ham; mix well. Sprinkle desired pizza crusts with *1 tablespoon* of the bread crumbs (see recipe, opposite). Spread meat mixture on crusts; sprinkle with remaining bread crumbs. Bake as directed in crust recipe.

3 Casseroles and Oven Favorites

You can enhance ground meats with pastas, spices, vegetables, cheeses, and pastry to make the delectable casseroles and oven-baked dishes in this chapter. The mealtime temptations shown are *Baked Mostaccioli, Individual Ham Puffs,* and *Sausage Zucchini Boats.* (See index for recipe pages.)

Casseroles

Meat-Noodle Casserole

3 ounces medium noodles
(2¼ cups)
1 10¾- *or* 11-ounce can
condensed soup*
½ cup dairy sour cream
½ cup milk
½ cup thinly sliced celery
1 2½-ounce jar sliced mushrooms,
drained
2 tablespoons chopped pimiento
1 tablespoon snipped parsley
1 pound ground meat, cooked and
drained**
Seasoning (optional)***
Crumbs****
¼ teaspoon paprika
(only for bread crumbs)
1 tablespoon butter *or*
margarine, melted

In large saucepan cook noodles in a large amount of boiling salted water for 10 to 12 minutes or just till tender; drain. Set aside. In large bowl stir together soup, sour cream, and milk. Add celery, mushrooms, pimiento, and parsley. Stir in cooked noodles, meat, and seasoning. Turn mixture into a 2-quart casserole. Combine crumbs and paprika (only with bread crumbs). Toss with melted butter or margarine; sprinkle over casserole. Bake, uncovered, in 375° oven for 30 to 35 minutes or till heated through. Makes 4 to 6 servings.

Soup suggestions: cream of mushroom, cream of celery, cream of chicken, cheddar cheese

**Meat suggestions* (cooked and drained): ground beef, ground pork, ground veal, ground lamb, ground raw turkey, bulk pork sausage

***Seasoning suggestions:* ¼ to ½ teaspoon chili powder (with beef or pork); ¼ teaspoon dried basil, crushed (with any meat); ¼ teaspoon dried oregano, crushed (with pork or sausage); ¼ teaspoon caraway seed (with pork or beef)

****Crumb suggestions:* ¾ cup soft bread crumbs (1 slice), ¾ cup coarsely crushed corn chips *or* tortilla chips (omit butter), ½ cup finely crushed saltine crackers (14 crackers), ½ cup finely crushed rich round crackers (12 crackers)

Grinding Your Own Meat

Making ground meat in a meat grinder or a food processor allows you to control the amount of fat. However, be sure to include some fat for flavor and juiciness.

For the grinder, cut meat into uniform size pieces, trimming all gristle and bone. The pieces should be slightly smaller than the grinder opening. Use a fine cutting plate to obtain a product similar to commercially ground meat.

In a food processor, process no more than ½ pound (1 cup) at a time to produce an evenly chopped mixture.

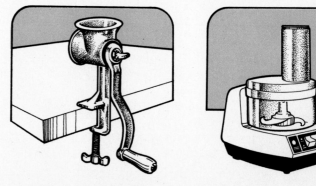

Ham-Macaroni Deluxe

1 beaten egg
⅓ cup milk
¼ cup soft bread crumbs
1 tablespoon prepared mustard
1 pound ground fully cooked ham
½ pound ground pork
1 cup elbow macaroni
½ cup chopped green pepper
2 tablespoons chopped onion
¼ cup butter *or* margarine
3 tablespoons all-purpose flour
2 cups milk
1 teaspoon worcestershire sauce
1½ cups shredded cheddar cheese
¼ cup finely crushed rich round
    crackers (6 crackers)
1 tablespoon butter, melted

In bowl combine egg and ⅓ cup milk. Stir in bread crumbs and mustard. Add ground ham and ground pork; mix well. In saucepan cook macaroni in boiling salted water about 10 minutes or just till tender. Drain; set aside. In saucepan cook green pepper and onion in ¼ cup butter or margarine till tender. Stir in flour. Add 2 cups milk and worcestershire sauce all at once; cook and stir till thickened and bubbly. Add cheese; stir till melted. Remove ¾ *cup* of the cheese mixture. Stir cooked macaroni into the remaining cheese mixture; turn into 12x7½x2-inch baking dish. Spoon meat mixture over top. Dot with the reserved ¾ cup cheese mixture.

Toss together cracker crumbs and 1 tablespoon melted butter; sprinkle buttered crumbs atop casserole. Bake, uncovered, in 350° oven about 40 minutes. Let stand 10 minutes before serving. Makes 8 servings.

Beef-Filled Corn Bread Squares

1 pound ground beef
⅓ cup chopped onion
1 clove garlic, minced
¼ cup catsup
1 10-ounce package corn bread
    mix
½ cup shredded American cheese
2 teaspoons cornstarch
1 7½-ounce can tomatoes, cut up
2 tablespoons chopped canned
    green chili peppers
2 tablespoons chopped green
    pepper
1 teaspoon worcestershire sauce

In skillet cook ground beef, onion, and garlic till meat is browned; drain off fat. Stir in catsup and ¾ teaspoon *salt*. In bowl prepare corn bread mix according to package directions. Spread *half* of the batter in a greased 8x8x2-inch baking pan. Spoon meat mixture over batter in pan; sprinkle with cheese. Spread remaining batter over cheese. Bake, uncovered, in 350° oven for 30 to 35 minutes. Let stand 5 minutes before cutting.

Meanwhile, in small saucepan combine cornstarch and 2 tablespoons *cold water*. Stir in *undrained* tomatoes, chili peppers, green pepper, and worcestershire. Cook and stir till thickened and bubbly. Cut corn bread into squares; serve tomato mixture atop. Makes 6 servings.

Freezing Casseroles

Your freezer can be helpful in planning and preparing meals. It gives you the flexibility of making casseroles ahead. (If you're serving one tonight, fix twice as much as you need and freeze the extra for a busy day.) Keep these hints in mind:

• Cool food quickly before wrapping for freezing. Set dish of hot food in ice water to cool.

• Before freezing cover casseroles with moisture-vaporproof material such as freezer paper, heavy foil, plastic wrap, or a tight-fitting lid.

• One handy way to freeze a casserole is to line the baking dish with heavy foil three times the length of the dish. Add prepared food and cool. Seal foil over food; freeze. When frozen, lift food, wrapped, from the dish and store it in the freezer. Return food to the same dish for reheating.

• Use frozen casseroles within 3 months for best quality.

Beef and Rice Espagnole

1 **pound ground beef** *or* **ground pork**
½ **cup chopped onion**
1 **15-ounce can tomato sauce**
½ **cup quick-cooking rice***
½ **cup water**
¼ **cup sliced pitted ripe olives**
1 **4-ounce can green chili peppers, rinsed, seeded, and chopped**
½ **teaspoon garlic salt**
⅛ **teaspoon pepper**
  Few drops bottled hot pepper sauce
1 **cup American cheese cut into ½-inch cubes**

In skillet cook meat and onion till meat is browned and onion is tender; drain off fat. Stir in tomato sauce, *uncooked* rice, water, olives, chili peppers, garlic salt, pepper, and hot pepper sauce. Bring to boiling.

Turn into a 1½-quart casserole. Cover; bake in 350° oven for 35 to 40 minutes or till rice is tender. Add cheese cubes, stirring just till cheese is distributed. Let stand 5 minutes before serving. Makes 4 to 6 servings.

Microwave cooking directions: In a 1½-quart nonmetal casserole crumble meat. Add onion. Cook, covered with waxed paper, in countertop microwave oven on high power for 6 to 8 minutes or till meat is browned and onion is tender. Stir once or twice to break up meat. Drain off fat. Stir in tomato sauce, *uncooked* rice*, *only ¼ cup water,* olives, chili peppers, garlic salt, pepper, and hot pepper sauce. Microcook, covered, for 10 to 12 minutes or till rice is tender, stirring after 4 minutes. Add cheese; stir just till distributed. Let stand 5 minutes before serving.

Note: Use Minute Rice when preparing in microwave oven.

Wild Rice-Pork Casserole

1 **6-ounce package long grain and wild rice mix**
1 **pound ground pork** *or* **ground beef**
½ **cup chopped celery**
½ **cup chopped onion**
1 **clove garlic, minced**
1 **11-ounce can condensed cheddar cheese soup**
½ **cup dairy sour cream**
½ **teaspoon ground sage**
¼ **cup snipped parsley** *or* **¼ cup toasted slivered almonds**

Prepare rice mix according to package directions. Meanwhile, in skillet cook ground pork or ground beef, celery, onion, and garlic till meat is browned and vegetables are tender. Drain off fat. Stir in soup, sour cream, and sage. Combine meat mixture and cooked rice. Turn into a 2-quart casserole. Bake, uncovered, in 350° oven for 35 to 40 minutes. Stir before serving; garnish with snipped parsley or toasted slivered almonds. Makes 6 servings.

Cheesy Beef-Rice Bake (pictured on page 74)

1 **pound ground beef** *or* **ground pork**
1 **clove garlic, minced**
1 **cup long grain rice**
2 **tablespoons butter** *or* **margarine**
3 **cups water**
1 **cup shredded carrot**
2 **teaspoons instant beef bouillon granules**
1 **teaspoon dried parsley flakes**
½ **teaspoon minced dried onion**
½ **teaspoon salt**
½ **teaspoon dried basil, crushed**
½ **cup shredded American cheese**

In large saucepan cook ground beef or ground pork and garlic till meat is browned. Drain off fat. Remove from pan and set aside. In same saucepan cook *uncooked* rice in butter or margarine till golden brown, stirring frequently. Stir in water, carrot, bouillon granules, parsley, dried onion, salt, and basil. Bring to boiling. Reduce heat; cover and simmer for 5 minutes. Stir in meat mixture.

Turn into a 1½-quart casserole. Cover; bake in 325° oven for 45 minutes, stirring twice. Sprinkle with shredded American cheese. Bake, uncovered, about 5 minutes longer or till cheese melts. Makes 6 servings.

Armenian Pilaf

1 pound ground lamb *or* ground
  beef
2 ounces fine noodles (1 cup)
2 tablespoons olive oil *or*
  cooking oil
3½ cups water
¾ cup long grain rice
½ cup raisins
1 tablespoon instant beef
  bouillon granules
½ teaspoon dried marjoram,
  crushed
¼ cup toasted slivered almonds

In skillet cook ground lamb or ground beef till browned. Drain off fat. Remove from pan and set aside. Wipe skillet. In same skillet brown *uncooked* noodles in hot olive or cooking oil till golden. Stir in meat, water, *uncooked* rice, raisins, beef bouillon granules, marjoram, and 1 teaspoon *salt*. Bring to boiling; turn into 2-quart casserole. Bake, covered, in 325° oven for 30 to 40 minutes or till liquid is absorbed, stirring once after 20 minutes. Sprinkle with toasted almonds. Makes 6 servings.

Turkey and Rice Squares

1½ teaspoons instant chicken
  bouillon granules
1¼ cups boiling water
½ cup brown rice
2 beaten eggs
1 10¾-ounce can condensed
  cream of mushroom soup
¼ cup milk
⅔ cup finely chopped celery
3 tablespoons chopped pimiento
1 teaspoon salt
¼ teaspoon dried rosemary,
  crushed
⅛ teaspoon pepper
4 cups coarsely ground *cooked*
  turkey *or* coarsely ground
  cooked chicken
  Mushroom Sauce

In saucepan dissolve chicken bouillon granules in boiling water. Cook rice in bouillon mixture about 1 hour or till tender. In bowl combine eggs, *half* of the mushroom soup (save remaining soup for Mushroom Sauce), and milk. Stir in cooked rice, celery, pimiento, salt, rosemary, and pepper. Add ground turkey or ground chicken; mix well. Pat firmly into 8x8x2-inch baking pan. Bake, uncovered, in 350° oven about 45 minutes or till center is firm. Let stand 5 to 10 minutes. Cut into squares. Serve with Mushroom Sauce. Makes 6 servings.

  Mushroom Sauce: In small saucepan combine ½ cup dairy *sour cream,* 2 tablespoons *milk,* ½ teaspoon *paprika,* and the remaining cream of mushroom soup. Cook and stir till mixture is heated through; *do not boil*.

Tamale Pie

1 pound ground beef
1 cup chopped onion
1 cup chopped green pepper
1 clove garlic, minced
1 15-ounce can tomato sauce
1 12-ounce can whole kernel
  corn, drained
½ cup sliced pitted ripe olives
1 tablespoon sugar
2 to 3 teaspoons chili powder
¾ teaspoon salt
  Dash pepper
1½ cups shredded American cheese
¾ cup yellow cornmeal
½ teaspoon salt
2 cups cold water

In skillet cook ground beef, onion, green pepper, and garlic till meat is browned and vegetables are tender. Drain off fat. Stir in tomato sauce, corn, olives, sugar, chili powder, ¾ teaspoon salt, and pepper. Boil gently for 20 to 25 minutes or till thickened, stirring occasionally. Add shredded American cheese; stir till melted. Turn mixture into a 2-quart casserole.

  In saucepan stir cornmeal and ½ teaspoon salt into cold water. Bring to boiling. Reduce heat; cook, stirring constantly, for ½ to 1 minute or till thickened. Spoon over hot meat mixture. Bake, uncovered, in 375° oven about 40 minutes. Makes 6 servings.

Baked Mostaccioli (pictured on pages 54 and 55)

8 ounces mostaccioli
1½ pounds ground beef
½ cup chopped onion
¼ cup chopped green pepper
1 clove garlic, minced
1 28-ounce can tomatoes, cut up
1 8-ounce can tomato sauce
1 6-ounce can tomato paste
1 4-ounce can mushroom stems
   and pieces
½ cup water
1 teaspoon salt
1 teaspoon sugar
1 teaspoon dried basil, crushed
⅛ teaspoon pepper
1 large bay leaf
6 ounces sliced mozzarella
   cheese
½ cup grated parmesan cheese

Cook mostaccioli in a large amount of boiling salted water about 14 minutes or just till tender; drain. Set aside. Meanwhile, in large saucepan cook ground beef, onion, green pepper, and garlic till meat is browned and vegetables are tender. Drain off fat. Stir in *undrained* tomatoes, tomato sauce, tomato paste, *undrained* mushrooms, water, salt, sugar, basil, pepper, and bay leaf. Bring to boiling; reduce heat. Cover; simmer for 30 minutes, stirring occasionally. Remove bay leaf. Stir in mostaccioli.

Turn *half* of the meat mixture into 3-quart casserole or 13x9x2-inch baking dish. Layer *half* of the mozzarella cheese atop. Top with remaining meat mixture. Sprinkle with parmesan cheese. Cover with foil. Bake in 350° oven about 35 minutes or till heated through. Remove foil. Cut remaining mozzarella cheese into strips; arrange atop casserole. Bake about 5 minutes more. Let stand 5 minutes before serving. Makes 8 to 10 servings.

Hamburger Pie

1 pound ground beef
½ cup chopped onion
1 16-ounce can cut green beans,
   drained
1 10¾-ounce can condensed
   tomato soup
¼ cup water
¾ teaspoon salt
⅛ teaspoon pepper
3 medium potatoes, peeled and
   quartered (1 pound)*
1 beaten egg
   Milk
½ cup shredded American cheese
   (2 ounces)

In large skillet cook ground beef and onion till meat is browned and onion is tender; drain off fat. Stir in green beans, tomato soup, water, salt, and pepper. Turn meat mixture into a 1½-quart casserole.

In covered pan cook potatoes in boiling salted water about 20 minutes or just till tender; drain.* Mash while hot; blend in egg. Add enough milk to make potatoes fluffy, yet stiff enough to hold their shape. Season with salt and pepper.

Drop potatoes in mounds atop meat mixture. Sprinkle with cheese. Bake, uncovered, in 350° oven for 25 to 30 minutes or till heated through. Makes 4 to 6 servings.

Note: Or, prepare packaged instant mashed potatoes (enough for 4 servings) according to package directions *except omit the milk*. Blend in the egg; add a little milk, if necessary, to make potatoes fluffy, yet stiff enough to hold their shape. Season with salt and pepper.

Pork and Noodle Casserole

4 ounces medium noodles (3 cups)
1 pound ground pork
1 small onion, chopped
1 16-ounce can stewed tomatoes
1 12-ounce can whole kernel
   corn, drained
1 6-ounce can tomato paste
1 teaspoon salt
1 teaspoon chili powder
¼ teaspoon garlic powder
   Dash pepper
1 cup shredded cheddar cheese

Cook noodles in a large amount of boiling salted water for 10 to 12 minutes or just till tender; drain. Meanwhile, in 10-inch skillet cook ground pork and onion till meat is browned and onion is tender; drain off fat. Stir in *undrained* tomatoes, corn, tomato paste, salt, chili powder, garlic powder, and pepper; mix well. Stir in noodles.

Turn mixture into a 1½-quart casserole. Cover and bake in 350° oven about 40 minutes or till heated through. Sprinkle with shredded cheese. Bake, uncovered, about 5 minutes more or till cheese is melted. Makes 6 servings.

You'll enjoy both of these meat-in-a-pie favorites—family-style *Hamburger Pie* and *Spaghetti Pie*, filled with beef or sausage, tomato, and cheese (see recipe, page 71).

Hamburger and Corn Casserole

3 ounces medium noodles
1 pound ground beef
½ cup chopped onion
1 10¾-ounce can condensed
   cream of chicken soup *or*
   cream of mushroom soup
1 8¾-ounce can whole kernel
   corn, drained
1 cup dairy sour cream
¼ cup milk
2 tablespoons chopped pimiento
½ teaspoon salt
   Dash pepper
1 cup soft bread crumbs
1 tablespoon butter *or*
   margarine, melted

Cook noodles in a large amount of boiling salted water for 10 to 12 minutes or just till tender; drain. Meanwhile, in large skillet cook ground beef and onion till meat is browned and onion is tender. Drain off fat. Stir in cream of chicken or mushroom soup, corn, sour cream, milk, pimiento, salt, and pepper; mix well. Stir in cooked noodles.

Turn mixture into a 1½-quart casserole. Toss together bread crumbs and melted butter or margarine; sprinkle atop casserole. Bake, uncovered, in 350° oven about 50 minutes or till heated through. Makes 4 or 5 servings.

Crowd-Size Hamburger Bake

4 pounds ground beef
3 cups chopped onion
1 cup chopped green pepper
16 ounces medium noodles
3 10¾-ounce cans condensed
   tomato soup
4 cups shredded American cheese
2 cups water
1 12-ounce bottle chili sauce
¼ cup chopped pimiento
2 teaspoons salt
2 teaspoons chili powder
½ teaspoon pepper
4½ cups soft bread crumbs
¼ cup butter, melted

In large skillet cook ground beef, onion, and green pepper, half at a time, till meat is browned. Drain off fat.

In large kettle cook noodles in a large amount of boiling salted water for 10 to 12 minutes or just till tender; drain well. Combine all of the meat mixture, tomato soup, shredded cheese, water, chili sauce, pimiento, salt, chili powder, and pepper; mix well. Fold in cooked noodles. Divide mixture between two 13x9x2-inch baking dishes.

Toss bread crumbs and melted butter; sprinkle atop casseroles. Bake, uncovered, in 350° oven about 45 minutes or till heated through. Garnish with green pepper rings, if desired. Makes 2 casseroles, 12 servings each.

Cottage Cheese-Beef Bake

3½ ounces medium noodles
1 pound ground beef *or* ground
   pork
½ cup chopped onion
¼ cup chopped green pepper
1 15-ounce can tomato sauce
½ teaspoon salt
½ teaspoon dried savory *or*
   marjoram, crushed
¼ teaspoon pepper
1½ cups cream-style cottage
   cheese (12 ounces)
1 3-ounce package cream cheese,
   softened
1 egg
¼ cup grated parmesan cheese

In large saucepan cook noodles in a large amount of boiling salted water for 10 to 12 minutes or just till tender; drain. In skillet cook ground beef or ground pork, onion, and green pepper till meat is browned and vegetables are tender; drain off fat. Stir in tomato sauce, salt, savory or marjoram, pepper, and the cooked noodles. Place *half* of the mixture in a 10x6x2-inch baking dish.

In small mixer bowl combine cottage cheese, cream cheese, and egg; beat till fluffy. Spread over meat mixture in baking dish. Top with the remaining meat mixture. Sprinkle with parmesan. Bake, uncovered, in 350° oven about 40 minutes or till heated through. Makes 6 servings.

Creamy Ham and Noodle Bake

4 ounces plain *or* green medium
    noodles
½ cup finely chopped onion
1 clove garlic, minced
2 tablespoons butter *or*
    margarine
3 hard-cooked eggs, chopped
2 cups small curd cream-style
    cottage cheese, drained
    (16 ounces)
1 cup dairy sour cream
⅓ cup grated parmesan cheese
1 teaspoon worcestershire sauce
¼ teaspoon salt
    Dash pepper
    Dash bottled hot pepper sauce
1 pound ground fully cooked ham
½ of a 3-ounce can French-fried
    onions
1 hard-cooked egg, quartered
    Parsley sprigs

In large saucepan cook plain or green noodles in a large amount of boiling salted water for 10 to 12 minutes or just till tender; drain. In skillet cook onion and garlic in butter or margarine till onion is tender but not brown. Combine onion mixture and the 3 chopped hard-cooked eggs; toss with drained noodles.

Place cottage cheese in blender container; cover and blend till smooth. Remove from blender. Combine cottage cheese, sour cream, parmesan cheese, worcestershire sauce, salt, pepper, and hot pepper sauce. Add ground ham; mix well. Fold into noodle mixture.

Turn into a 13x9x2-inch baking dish. Bake, uncovered, in 350° oven for 20 minutes. Sprinkle the French-fried onions around edges of casserole. Bake, uncovered, about 5 minutes more. Garnish with quartered hard-cooked egg and parsley sprigs. Pass additional grated parmesan cheese, if desired. Makes 8 servings.

Tostada Bake

1 pound ground beef
½ teaspoon garlic salt
6 cups corn chips, coarsely
    crushed (10 ounces)
4 or 5 slices American cheese
2 cups shredded lettuce
    Homemade Taco Sauce

In skillet cook ground beef till browned, drain off fat. Stir in garlic salt. Place corn chips in 8x8x2-inch baking dish or 8x1½-inch round baking dish. Spoon hot meat over corn chips; top with cheese slices. Bake, uncovered, in 350° oven for 10 to 12 minutes or till heated through and cheese is melted. Sprinkle casserole with shredded lettuce; spoon on Homemade Taco Sauce. Makes 4 to 6 servings.

Homemade Taco Sauce: In mixing bowl stir together one 16-ounce can *stewed tomatoes,* undrained; 1 teaspoon *sugar;* ¾ teaspoon dried *oregano,* crushed; ½ teaspoon *worcestershire sauce;* ¼ teaspoon *salt;* ¼ teaspoon bottled *hot pepper sauce;* and ⅛ teaspoon *pepper.* Using the edge of a spoon, break up large tomato pieces. Stir in ¼ cup chopped *onion* and ¼ cup chopped *green pepper.*

Chili-Spaghetti Dinner for Two

½ pound bulk pork sausage
¼ cup chopped onion
¼ cup chopped carrot
1¼ cups tomato juice
1 8-ounce can red kidney beans,
    drained
½ teaspoon salt
½ teaspoon chili powder
    Dash pepper
½ cup broken spaghetti

In saucepan cook sausage, onion, and carrot till meat is browned. Drain off fat. Stir in tomato juice, kidney beans, salt, chili powder, and pepper. Place *uncooked* spaghetti in a 1-quart casserole; stir in meat mixture. Bake, uncovered, in 375° oven for 55 to 60 minutes or till spaghetti is tender, stirring twice. Makes 2 or 3 servings.

Individual Vegetable-Meat Casseroles

 1 **pound bulk pork sausage** *or*
   ground beef
 ½ **cup chopped onion**
 3 **tablespoons all-purpose flour**
 1 **16-ounce can tomatoes, cut up**
 1 **10-ounce package frozen whole**
   kernel corn, thawed, *or* **one**
   17-ounce can whole kernel
   corn, drained
 1 **9-ounce package frozen cut**
   green beans, thawed, *or* **one**
   16-ounce can cut green
   beans, drained
 1 **cup all-purpose flour**
 2 **teaspoons baking powder**
 ¼ **teaspoon dried thyme, crushed,**
   or **ground sage**
 ½ **cup milk**
 2 **tablespoons cooking oil**
 ⅓ **cup shredded sharp cheddar**
   cheese

In large skillet cook sausage or ground beef and onion till meat is browned and onion is tender; drain off fat. Stir in the 3 tablespoons flour, ½ teaspoon *salt,* and dash *pepper.* Stir in *undrained* tomatoes. Cook, stirring constantly, till thickened and bubbly. Stir in corn and green beans. Bring mixture to boiling.

Meanwhile, to make dumplings, in a medium mixing bowl thoroughly stir together the 1 cup flour, baking powder, thyme or sage, and ½ teaspoon *salt.* In another bowl combine milk and cooking oil. Add milk mixture all at once to flour mixture, stirring just till moistened.

Spoon boiling-hot meat mixture into six 8-ounce individual casseroles. Drop dumpling dough from a tablespoon onto each casserole. Sprinkle *each* with about *1 tablespoon* shredded cheddar cheese. Bake, uncovered, in 350° oven for 25 to 30 minutes. Makes 6 servings.

Ham and Mushroom Bake

 2½ **ounces medium noodles**
 ⅓ **cup chopped onion**
 1 **teaspoon curry powder**
 2 **tablespoons butter** *or*
   margarine
 3 **tablespoons all-purpose flour**
 ½ **teaspoon salt**
 1¾ **cups milk**
 1 **10-ounce package frozen peas,**
   thawed
 1 **pound ground fully cooked ham**
 1 **2-ounce can chopped**
   mushrooms, drained
 ½ **cup coarsely crushed rich**
   round crackers
 1 **tablespoon butter** *or*
   margarine, melted

In large saucepan cook noodles in a large amount of boiling salted water for 10 to 12 minutes or just till tender; drain. Meanwhile, in saucepan cook onion and curry powder in the 2 tablespoons butter or margarine till onion is tender. Stir in flour and salt. Add milk all at once; cook and stir till thickened and bubbly. Stir in peas; remove from heat. Stir in ground ham and mushrooms. Gently fold in noodles.

Turn mixture into a 2-quart casserole. Toss together cracker crumbs and the 1 tablespoon melted butter; sprinkle atop casserole. Bake, uncovered, in 350° oven for 30 to 35 minutes or till heated through. Makes 6 servings.

Easy Cassoulet

 ½ **pound bulk pork sausage**
 1 **small onion, sliced**
 1 **clove garlic, minced**
 2 **15-ounce cans navy beans**
 1½ **cups cubed fully cooked ham**
 ¼ **cup dry white wine**
 2 **tablespoons snipped parsley**
 1 **bay leaf**
   Dash ground cloves

In skillet cook sausage, onion, and garlic till meat is browned and onion is tender; drain off fat. Stir in *undrained* navy beans, cubed ham, white wine, parsley, bay leaf, and cloves. Turn mixture into a 1½-quart casserole. Cover and bake in 325° oven for 45 minutes. Uncover; bake for 40 to 45 minutes more, stirring occasionally. Remove bay leaf. Serve in bowls. Makes 6 servings.

Savory Sausage Casserole

6 ounces wide noodles (3 cups)
1 pound bulk pork sausage *or* bulk Italian sausage
½ cup chopped green pepper
½ cup chopped celery
½ cup chopped carrot
1 10¾-ounce can condensed cream of celery soup
⅓ cup milk
¼ cup mayonnaise *or* salad dressing
½ teaspoon dried oregano, crushed
1 cup shredded mozzarella *or* provolone cheese (4 ounces)
⅓ cup fine dry bread crumbs
2 tablespoons butter *or* margarine, melted
Snipped parsley

In large saucepan cook noodles in a large amount of boiling salted water about 12 minutes or just till tender; drain. Meanwhile, in large skillet cook sausage, green pepper, celery, and carrot till meat is browned and vegetables are tender. Drain off fat. In mixing bowl combine cream of celery soup, milk, mayonnaise or salad dressing, and oregano. Stir in sausage mixture and mozzarella or provolone cheese. Gently fold in drained noodles.

Turn into a 2-quart casserole. Toss together bread crumbs and melted butter or margarine; sprinkle atop casserole. Bake, uncovered, in 350° oven for 45 to 50 minutes or till heated through. Garnish with parsley. Makes 4 to 6 servings.

Pork Strata

1 pound ground pork
½ cup chopped onion
¼ cup chopped green pepper
1 2-ounce can chopped mushrooms, drained
¼ teaspoon salt
5 cups dry bread cubes
4 beaten eggs
1 10¾-ounce can condensed cream of mushroom soup
1¼ cups milk
½ cup mayonnaise *or* salad dressing
¾ teaspoon dried thyme, crushed
¼ teaspoon cayenne
2 tablespoons butter *or* margarine, melted

In skillet cook ground pork, onion, and green pepper till meat is browned; drain off fat. Stir mushrooms and salt into meat mixture. Place *2 cups* of the bread cubes in a 12x7½x2-inch baking dish. Spoon meat mixture over bread in dish. Add another *2 cups* of the bread cubes. Combine eggs, cream of mushroom soup, milk, mayonnaise or salad dressing, thyme, and cayenne. Pour over ingredients in baking dish. Cover and refrigerate at least 1 hour.

Toss together the remaining bread cubes and melted butter or margarine; sprinkle atop casserole. Bake, uncovered, in 325° oven about 50 minutes or till nearly set. Let stand 10 minutes before serving. Makes 8 servings.

Individual Ham Puffs (pictured on pages 54 and 55)

4 eggs
½ cup milk
½ teaspoon dry mustard
⅛ teaspoon pepper
2 3-ounce packages cream cheese, cut up
4 ounces brick cheese, cut up
1 cup ground fully cooked ham
½ teaspoon dried parsley flakes

In blender container combine eggs, milk, dry mustard, and pepper. Cover and blend till smooth. With blender running, add cheeses through opening in lid or with lid ajar. Blend till cheese mixture is nearly smooth. Stir in ground ham and dried parsley flakes. Pour mixture into four *ungreased* 1-cup soufflé dishes. Bake in 375° oven for 25 to 30 minutes or till set. Makes 4 servings.

Serves-a-Dozen Lasagne

1 pound bulk Italian sausage
½ cup chopped onion
½ cup chopped celery
½ cup chopped carrot
1 clove garlic, minced
1 16-ounce can tomatoes, cut up
1 6-ounce can tomato paste
1 teaspoon sugar
1 teaspoon dried oregano, crushed
½ teaspoon fennel seed
   Dash bottled hot pepper sauce
10 ounces lasagne noodles
2 beaten eggs
2 cups ricotta *or* cream-style cottage cheese
½ cup grated parmesan cheese
2 tablespoons snipped parsley
8 ounces mozzarella cheese

In 10-inch skillet cook Italian sausage, onion, celery, carrot, and garlic till meat is browned. Drain off fat. Stir in *undrained* tomatoes, tomato paste, sugar, oregano, fennel seed, hot pepper sauce, 1 teaspoon *salt,* and ¼ teaspoon *pepper.* Bring mixture to boiling; reduce heat. Cover and simmer for 20 minutes, stirring occasionally.

Meanwhile, cook lasagne noodles in a large amount of boiling salted water for 10 to 12 minutes or till tender; drain. Rinse in cold water; drain. Combine eggs, ricotta or cottage cheese, parmesan cheese, parsley, and ¼ teaspoon *pepper.* Thinly slice mozzarella cheese.

Arrange *half* of the lasagne noodles in bottom of a greased 13x9x2-inch baking dish. Spread with *half* of the ricotta mixture; top with the mozzarella cheese and *half* of the meat sauce. Repeat the layers of noodles, ricotta mixture, and meat sauce. Bake, uncovered, in 375° oven about 40 minutes or till heated through. Let stand 10 minutes before serving. Makes 12 servings.

Herbed Beef and Cavatelli Bake

3 ounces cavatelli *or* elbow macaroni (about 1 cup)
½ pound ground beef
½ pound bulk pork sausage
1 cup chopped fresh mushrooms
½ cup chopped onion
1 clove garlic, minced
1 16-ounce can tomatoes, cut up
1 10½-ounce can tomato puree
¼ cup dry red wine
1 bay leaf
1½ teaspoons dried basil, crushed
1 teaspoon dried oregano, crushed
½ teaspoon crushed red pepper
¾ cup shredded provolone cheese

Cook cavatelli or macaroni in a large amount of boiling salted water for 10 to 12 minutes or just till tender; drain. Meanwhile, in large skillet cook ground beef, sausage, mushrooms, onion, and garlic till meat is browned and onion is tender. Drain off fat. Stir in *undrained* tomatoes, tomato puree, wine, bay leaf, basil, oregano, red pepper, and ¼ teaspoon *salt.* Bring to boiling; reduce heat. Boil gently, uncovered, for 10 minutes, stirring occasionally. Discard bay leaf. Stir in drained pasta.

Turn mixture into a 10x6x2-inch baking dish. Bake, uncovered, in 350° oven for 20 minutes. Sprinkle with cheese. Return to oven; bake, uncovered, about 5 minutes more or till cheese is melted. Makes 4 to 6 servings.

Green Bean Moussaka

1 pound ground beef
1 tablespoon all-purpose flour
1 8-ounce can tomato sauce
½ teaspoon garlic salt
¼ teaspoon ground cinnamon
1 16-ounce can French-style *or* cut green beans, drained
2 beaten eggs
1½ cups cream-style cottage cheese with chives
¼ cup grated parmesan cheese

In skillet cook ground beef till browned; drain off fat. Stir in flour. Stir in tomato sauce, garlic salt, and cinnamon. Place green beans in a 10x6x2-inch baking dish. Spread the meat mixture atop. Combine eggs and cottage cheese; spoon over meat mixture. Sprinkle with parmesan cheese. Bake, uncovered, in 375° oven about 25 minutes or till heated through. If desired, sprinkle with sliced pitted ripe olives. Makes 6 servings.

Manicotti

8 **manicotti shells**
1 **pound ground beef** *or* **bulk Italian sausage**
2 **cups water**
2 **6-ounce cans tomato paste**
½ **cup chopped onion**
⅓ **cup snipped parsley**
1 **large clove garlic, minced**
1 **tablespoon dried basil, crushed**
1½ **teaspoons salt**
Dash pepper
2 **beaten eggs**
3 **cups ricotta** *or* **cream-style cottage cheese, drained**
¾ **cup grated romano** *or* **parmesan cheese**
¼ **teaspoon salt**
Dash pepper

Cook manicotti shells in a large amount of boiling salted water about 18 minutes or till tender; drain. Rinse shells in cold water; drain. Meanwhile, in large saucepan cook ground beef or sausage till browned; drain off fat. Stir in water, tomato paste, onion, *half* of the parsley, garlic, basil, the 1½ teaspoons salt, and dash pepper. Bring mixture to boiling; reduce heat. Simmer, uncovered, for 15 minutes, stirring mixture occasionally.

In bowl combine eggs, ricotta or cottage cheese, *½ cup* of the romano or parmesan cheese, the ¼ teaspoon salt, dash pepper, and the remaining parsley. Stuff cooked manicotti shells with cheese mixture.

Pour *half* of the meat mixture into a 12x7½x2-inch baking dish. Arrange stuffed manicotti in baking dish; top with remaining meat mixture. Sprinkle with remaining romano or parmesan cheese. Bake, uncovered, in 350° oven for 40 to 45 minutes or till heated through. Let stand 10 minutes before serving. Makes 6 to 8 servings.

Moussaka

2 **medium eggplants (1½ to 2 pounds total)**
½ **pound ground beef**
½ **pound ground lamb**
1 **cup chopped onion**
⅓ **cup tomato paste**
¼ **cup snipped parsley**
¼ **cup dry red wine**
¼ **cup water**
2 **beaten eggs**
¼ **cup grated parmesan cheese**
¼ **cup fine dry bread crumbs**
¾ **teaspoon salt**
½ **teaspoon ground cinnamon**
⅛ **teaspoon pepper**
¼ **cup butter** *or* **margarine**
¼ **cup all-purpose flour**
¼ **teaspoon salt**
Dash ground nutmeg
Dash pepper
2 **cups milk**
2 **beaten egg yolks**
2 **tablespoons lemon juice**
Cooking oil
¼ **cup fine dry bread crumbs**
2 **tablespoons grated parmesan cheese**
1 **tablespoon butter** *or* **margarine, melted**

Peel eggplants; cut crosswise into ¾-inch-thick slices. Sprinkle slices with a little salt; set aside. In skillet cook ground beef, ground lamb, and onion till meat is browned and onion is tender. Drain off fat. Stir in tomato paste, parsley, red wine, and water. Simmer, uncovered, for 5 minutes; cool. Stir in the 2 eggs, the ¼ cup parmesan cheese, the ¼ cup bread crumbs, the ¾ teaspoon salt, cinnamon, and the ⅛ teaspoon pepper. Set aside.

In medium saucepan melt the ¼ cup butter or margarine. Stir in flour, the ¼ teaspoon salt, nutmeg, and dash pepper. Add milk all at once; cook and stir till mixture is thickened and bubbly. Stir about *1 cup* of the hot mixture into egg yolks; return to remaining hot mixture in saucepan. Cook and stir for 2 minutes more. Remove from heat; gradually stir in lemon juice. Set aside.

In large skillet brown eggplant slices in a little hot oil, about 1½ minutes on each side. Drain on paper toweling. Sprinkle bottom of a greased 12x7½x2-inch baking dish with *2 tablespoons* of the remaining bread crumbs. Layer with *half* of the eggplant. Spread with meat mixture; top with the remaining eggplant. Pour milk mixture over all. Cover and bake in 350° oven for 45 minutes. Combine the remaining 2 tablespoons bread crumbs, the 2 tablespoons parmesan cheese, and the 1 tablespoon melted butter or margarine; sprinkle atop casserole. Bake about 15 minutes more. Makes 6 servings.

Start with pork sausage, fresh vegetables, cream, and cheeses to create rich-tasting
Sausage Quiche. To complete a light meal, just add a crisp green salad and a glass of wine.

Sausage Quiche

Plain Pastry for a single-
crust pie (see recipe, below)
½ pound bulk pork sausage
¾ cup sliced fresh mushrooms
¼ cup chopped onion
¼ cup chopped green pepper
1 clove garlic, minced
3 beaten eggs
1½ cups light cream *or* milk
1 tablespoon all-purpose flour
¼ teaspoon salt
Dash pepper
¾ cup shredded mozzarella
cheese
¼ cup grated parmesan cheese
1 tablespoon snipped parsley

Prepare and roll out pastry. Line a 9-inch quiche dish or pie plate; trim pastry to ½ inch beyond edge. Flute edge high. *Do not* prick crust. Line with double thickness heavy-duty foil. Bake in 450° oven for 5 minutes. Remove foil; bake for 5 to 7 minutes more. Remove from oven; reduce oven temperature to 325°. (Pie shell should be hot when filling is added; do not partially bake ahead of time.)

Meanwhile, in skillet cook sausage till browned. Drain well, reserving *1 tablespoon* drippings. Set sausage aside. Cook mushrooms, onion, green pepper, and garlic in reserved drippings till tender. Remove from heat; set aside.

Combine eggs, cream or milk, flour, salt, and pepper. Sprinkle sausage over warm pastry; top with mushroom mixture. Place on rack in oven; gently pour egg mixture over mushroom mixture. Sprinkle with mozzarella cheese; top with parmesan cheese and parsley. Bake in 325° oven for 45 to 50 minutes or till almost set in center. If necessary, cover edge of crust with foil to prevent overbrowning. Let stand 10 minutes before serving. Makes 6 servings.

Pizza Pie

Plain Pastry for a double-crust
pie (see recipe, below)
4 ounces bulk Italian sausage
3 eggs
1 cup ricotta *or* cream-
style cottage cheese
1 cup shredded mozzarella
cheese
½ cup sliced pepperoni, halved
½ cup cubed prosciutto *or* fully
cooked ham
¼ cup grated parmesan cheese
1 beaten egg
2 tablespoons milk

Prepare and roll out only *half* of the pastry to a 12-inch circle; reserve the remaining pastry. Fit pastry circle into a 9-inch pie plate. Trim to ½ inch beyond edge of pie plate. Fold under and flute edge; *do not* prick crust. Bake in 450° oven for 5 minutes. Remove from oven; reduce oven temperature to 350°. Cook Italian sausage till browned; drain well. Beat together the 3 eggs and ricotta or cottage cheese. Fold in next 4 ingredients and Italian sausage. Turn into pastry shell.

Roll out remaining pastry dough to an 8-inch circle; cut into 6 to 8 wedges. Arrange wedges atop filling. Bake in 350° oven for 20 minutes. Combine the 1 beaten egg and milk; brush over wedges. Bake about 20 minutes more or till golden. Let stand 10 minutes. Makes 6 to 8 servings.

Plain Pastry

1 cup all-purpose flour
½ teaspoon salt
⅓ cup shortening *or* lard
3 to 4 tablespoons cold water

Stir together flour and salt; cut in shortening or lard till pieces are the size of small peas. Sprinkle *1 tablespoon* of the water over part of the mixture; gently toss with a fork. Push to side of bowl. Repeat till all is moistened.

For single-crust pie: Form dough into a ball. Flatten on lightly floured surface. Roll dough from center to edge, forming a circle about 12 inches in diameter. Fit pastry into a 9-inch pie plate. Trim to ½ inch beyond edge of plate. Fold under and flute edge. Continue as directed in recipe.

For double-crust pie: Prepare dough as directed above *except* double the recipe. Form into two balls. Flatten each on lightly floured surface. Roll each from center to edge, forming a circle about 12 inches in diameter. Fit one circle into 9-inch pie plate. Continue as directed in recipe.

Beef and Broccoli Pie

Plain Pastry for a double-crust
    pie (see recipe, page 69)
1 pound ground beef *or* bulk pork
    sausage
¼ cup chopped onion
2 tablespoons all-purpose flour
¾ teaspoon salt
¼ teaspoon garlic salt
1¼ cups milk
1 3-ounce package cream cheese,
    softened
1 beaten egg
1 10-ounce package frozen
    chopped broccoli, cooked and
    well drained
4 ounces sliced monterey jack,
    American, *or* Swiss cheese
    Milk
    Parsley sprigs (optional)
    Carrot curls (optional)

Prepare and roll out pastry. Line a 9-inch pie plate with *half* of the pastry. Trim pastry even with rim of pie plate. In skillet cook ground beef or sausage and onion till meat is browned and onion is tender; drain off fat. Stir in flour, salt, and garlic salt. Add the 1¼ cups milk and cream cheese. Cook, stirring constantly, till smooth and bubbly. Stir about *1 cup* of the hot mixture into the beaten egg; return to remaining hot mixture in skillet. Cook and stir over medium heat for 1 to 2 minutes more; *do not boil*. Stir in cooked and drained broccoli.

Spoon the hot meat mixture into pastry-lined pie plate. Arrange cheese slices atop meat mixture. For top crust cut slits in second pastry circle for escape of steam; place pastry atop filling. Seal and flute edge. Brush pastry with a little additional milk. To prevent overbrowning, cover edge of crust with foil. Bake in 350° oven for 20 minutes. Remove foil and bake for 20 to 25 minutes more or till crust is golden brown. Let stand 10 minutes before serving. Garnish with parsley sprigs and carrot curls, if desired. Makes 6 servings.

French-Canadian Pork Pie

1 pound ground pork
1 cup water
1 medium onion, finely chopped
    (½ cup)
½ cup fine dry bread crumbs
    (2 slices)
1 teaspoon salt
⅛ teaspoon ground sage
    Dash ground nutmeg
    Dash pepper
    Plain Pastry for a double-crust
    pie (see recipe, page 69)

In skillet cook ground pork till meat is browned; drain off fat. Stir in water, onion, bread crumbs, salt, sage, nutmeg, and pepper. Bring to boiling; reduce heat. Cover and simmer about 20 minutes or till onion is tender, stirring often.

Meanwhile, prepare and roll out pastry. Line a 9-inch pie plate with *half* of the pastry. Trim pastry even with rim of pie plate. Spoon hot meat mixture into pastry-lined pie plate. For top crust cut slits in second pastry circle for escape of steam; place pastry atop filling. Seal and flute edge. Bake in 400° oven about 30 minutes or till crust is golden brown. If necessary, cover edge of crust with foil to prevent overbrowning. Makes 6 servings.

Pork and Apple Pie

Plain Pastry for a double-crust
    pie (see recipe, page 69)
1 pound ground pork
1 medium onion, finely chopped
    (½ cup)
½ cup fine dry bread crumbs
½ cup water
1 teaspoon salt
½ teaspoon instant chicken
    bouillon granules
    Dash pepper
2 medium cooking apples, peeled,
    cored, and sliced (2 cups)
2 tablespoons brown sugar
¼ teaspoon ground cinnamon

Prepare and roll out pastry. Line a 9-inch pie plate with *half* of the pastry. Trim pastry even with rim of pie plate. In skillet cook ground pork and onion till meat is browned and onion is tender; drain off fat. Stir in bread crumbs, water, salt, bouillon granules, and pepper. Spoon hot meat mixture into pastry-lined pie plate.

Combine sliced apples, brown sugar, and cinnamon; spoon atop meat layer. For top crust cut slits in second pastry circle for escape of steam; place pastry atop filling. Seal and flute edge. Bake in 400° oven for 35 to 40 minutes or till crust is golden brown. Let pie stand for 10 minutes before serving. Makes 6 servings.

Greek-Style Crepe Casserole

16 **Main Dish Crepes (see recipe, page 90)**
1½ **pounds ground beef *or* ground lamb**
1 **cup chopped onion**
1 **16-ounce can tomatoes, cut up**
1 **6-ounce can tomato paste**
1 **teaspoon salt**
¼ **teaspoon dried thyme, crushed**
4 **slightly beaten egg whites**
½ **cup cubed feta cheese *or* American cheese**
½ **cup butter *or* margarine**
½ **cup all-purpose flour**
1 **teaspoon salt**
¼ **teaspoon ground cinnamon**
4 **cups milk**
4 **slightly beaten egg yolks**

Prepare Main Dish Crepes; set aside. For filling, in skillet cook ground beef or ground lamb and onion till meat is browned and onion is tender. Drain off fat. Stir in *undrained* tomatoes, tomato paste, 1 teaspoon salt, and thyme. Cover and simmer for 25 to 30 minutes, stirring frequently. Stir about *half* of the hot mixture into egg whites; return to remaining hot mixture in skillet. Cook and stir for 1 to 2 minutes more. Remove from heat; stir in cubed cheese.

Meanwhile, for sauce, in saucepan melt butter or margarine. Stir in flour, 1 teaspoon salt, and cinnamon; add milk. Cook and stir till thickened and bubbly. Remove from heat. Gradually stir about *half* of the hot mixture into egg yolks; return to remaining hot mixture, stirring rapidly.

Spread *half* of the filling in a 13x9x2-inch baking dish. Arrange eight Main Dish Crepes atop, overlapping to fit dish. Repeat the layers of filling and crepes. Pour sauce over crepes. Sprinkle lightly with additional cinnamon, if desired. Bake, uncovered, in 375° oven about 25 minutes or till heated through and top is set. Let stand 10 minutes before serving. Makes 10 to 12 servings.

Taco Casserole

1 **pound ground beef**
½ **cup chopped onion**
1 **clove garlic, minced**
¾ **teaspoon salt**
⅛ **teaspoon pepper**
1 **10-ounce can enchilada sauce**
1 **8-ounce can tomato sauce**
1½ **teaspoons instant coffee crystals**
12 **corn tortillas**
1 **3-ounce package cream cheese, softened**
1½ **cups shredded American cheese**

In skillet cook ground beef, onion, garlic, salt, and pepper till meat is browned and onion is tender; drain off fat. Combine enchilada sauce and tomato sauce. Stir *1 cup* of the sauce mixture and the coffee crystals into meat mixture.

Spread one side of each tortilla with some of the softened cream cheese; place about ¼ cup of the meat mixture in center of *each* tortilla. Sprinkle tortillas with *1 cup* of the shredded American cheese. Fold tortillas in half. Place, open side up, in 12x7½x2-inch baking dish. Combine the remaining sauce mixture and ½ cup *water;* pour over tortillas. Bake, covered, in 375° oven for 25 minutes. Uncover; sprinkle with remaining ½ cup American cheese. Bake for 2 to 3 minutes more or till cheese is melted. Makes 6 servings.

Hearty Mexican Casserole

1 **pound ground beef**
¼ **cup chopped onion**
¾ **cup finely chopped fully cooked ham**
¼ **cup taco sauce**
1 **1¼-ounce envelope taco seasoning mix**
1 **10-ounce package frozen chopped spinach**
 Cooking oil
12 **corn tortillas**
1 **cup dairy sour cream**
1 **cup shredded monterey jack cheese (4 ounces)**

In skillet cook ground beef and onion till meat is browned and onion is tender. Drain off fat. Stir in ham, taco sauce, dry taco seasoning mix, 1 cup *water,* and ¼ teaspoon *salt.* Top with frozen spinach. Cover and cook till spinach is thawed, breaking up spinach with a fork. Cover and simmer for 5 minutes more. In small skillet heat a little oil. Dip tortillas, one at a time, into hot oil for 5 to 10 seconds or just till limp. Drain on paper toweling.

Spoon about ⅓ cup of the meat mixture down center of *each* tortilla; roll up. Place tortillas, seam side down, in greased 13x9x2-inch baking dish. Cover and bake in 350° oven for 30 to 35 minutes or till heated through. Uncover; spread sour cream over tortillas. Sprinkle with cheese. Bake for 5 to 10 minutes more. Makes 6 servings.

These hearty oven dishes include flavorful *Cheesy Beef-Rice Bake* (see recipe, page 58) and Greek-style *Pastitsio* layered with pasta, spiced meat, and parmesan-flavored custard.

Pastitsio

- 6 ounces elbow macaroni
    (1½ cups)
- 1 beaten egg
- ⅓ cup grated parmesan cheese
- ¼ cup milk
- 1 pound ground lamb *or* ground
    beef
- ½ cup chopped onion
- 1 8-ounce can tomato sauce
- ½ teaspoon ground cinnamon
- ⅛ teaspoon ground nutmeg
- 3 tablespoons butter *or*
    margarine
- 3 tablespoons all-purpose flour
- 1½ cups milk
- 1 beaten egg
- ¼ cup grated parmesan cheese

Cook macaroni in a large amount of boiling salted water about 10 minutes or just till tender; drain. Combine cooked macaroni, 1 beaten egg, the ⅓ cup parmesan cheese, and the ¼ cup milk; set aside. In skillet cook ground lamb or ground beef and onion till meat is browned and onion is tender; drain off fat. Stir in tomato sauce, cinnamon, nutmeg, ½ teaspoon *salt,* and ⅛ teaspoon *pepper;* set aside.

For sauce, in saucepan melt butter or margarine; stir in flour and ¼ teaspoon *salt.* Add the 1½ cups milk all at once; cook and stir till thickened and bubbly. Remove from heat. Stir about *half* of the hot mixture into 1 beaten egg; return to remaining hot mixture in saucepan. Stir in the ¼ cup grated parmesan cheese.

Place *half* of the macaroni mixture in an 8x8x2-inch baking dish. Spoon the meat mixture atop; add the remaining macaroni mixture. Spread the sauce over all. Bake, uncovered, in 350° oven for 40 to 45 minutes. Let stand 10 minutes before serving. Makes 6 servings.

Ground Beef Curry with Custard Topping

- 2 pounds ground beef
- 1 cup chopped onion
- 2 tablespoons curry powder
- 2 beaten eggs
- ½ cup milk
- 1½ cups soft bread crumbs
- ½ cup raisins
- ½ cup chopped blanched almonds
- 2 tablespoons vinegar
- 4 bay leaves, crushed
- 1 tablespoon sugar
- 1 teaspoon salt
- ⅛ teaspoon pepper
- 3 beaten eggs
- ⅔ cup milk
- ⅛ teaspoon salt

In large skillet cook ground beef, onion, and curry powder till meat is browned; drain off fat. Remove from heat. Stir in the 2 beaten eggs and the ½ cup milk; stir in bread crumbs, raisins, almonds, vinegar, bay leaves, sugar, the 1 teaspoon salt, and pepper.

Press meat mixture into a 9x9x2-inch baking pan. Combine the 3 eggs, the ⅔ cup milk, ⅛ teaspoon salt, and dash *pepper;* beat just till blended. Slowly pour over meat mixture. Bake, uncovered, in 350° oven about 45 minutes or till top is set and lightly browned. Makes 8 servings.

Turkey Hash Bake

- 2 slices bacon
- 1 pound ground raw turkey
- ¼ cup finely chopped onion
- 1 cup finely chopped cooked
    potato
- 1 5⅓-ounce can evaporated milk
- 3 tablespoons snipped parsley
- 2 teaspoons worcestershire sauce
- ¼ teaspoon ground sage
- ¼ cup finely crushed rich round
    crackers (6 crackers)
- 1 tablespoon butter *or*
    margarine, melted

In skillet cook bacon till crisp; drain. Crumble bacon and set aside. In skillet cook ground turkey and onion till meat is browned. Drain off fat. In bowl combine turkey mixture, potato, evaporated milk, parsley, worcestershire sauce, sage, ¾ teaspoon *salt,* and dash *pepper.* Turn mixture into a 1-quart casserole.

Toss together cracker crumbs and melted butter or margarine; sprinkle atop casserole. Bake in 375° oven for 20 to 25 minutes. Sprinkle with bacon. Bake about 5 minutes more or till heated through. Makes 4 servings.

4 Skillet Dishes and Other Specialties

Expand the limits of ground meats by including them in one-dish meals, meat sauces, omelets, and crepes. Among the recipes in this chapter you'll find *South of the Border Salad, Ham Croquettes with Cheese Sauce,* and *Olive Spaghetti Sauce.* (See index for recipe pages.)

Skillet Dishes

Frozen Beef Starter

3 beaten eggs
2 cups soft bread crumbs
   (about 3 slices)
1 cup chopped celery
1 cup chopped onion
1 cup shredded carrot
1 teaspoon salt
3 pounds ground beef

Combine eggs, bread crumbs, celery, onion, carrot, and salt. Add meat; mix well. In large skillet cook half the mixture at a time till meat is lightly browned. Stir to break up large pieces of meat. Drain off fat. Cool quickly. Seal in 2-cup portions in moisture-vaporproof containers or freezer bags. Label; freeze. Use as directed in recipes below and on opposite page. Makes five 2-cup portions.

Note: In recipes that use Frozen Beef Starter, if desired substitute *1 pound ground beef* for *2 cups* starter. To prepare meat, cook ground beef with ⅓ cup chopped *onion* till browned; drain off fat. Stir in ¼ teaspoon *salt.* Continue as directed in recipe *except* omit thawing instructions.

Meat and Mac Skillet (pictured on page 80)

1 cup elbow macaroni
2 cups Frozen Beef Starter (see
   recipe, above)
1 8¾-ounce can whole kernel corn
2 tablespoons snipped parsley
1 teaspoon chili powder
½ teaspoon garlic salt
¼ teaspoon ground cumin
1 8-ounce package cream cheese,
   softened
¾ cup milk
2 medium tomatoes
2 slices American cheese, halved
   diagonally

In saucepan cook macaroni in a large amount of boiling salted water about 10 minutes or just till tender. Drain and set aside. To thaw Frozen Beef Starter, in skillet combine frozen meat mixture and ¼ cup *water*. Cover and cook over low heat for 15 minutes; break up meat with fork. Cover; cook 5 minutes more. Drain corn. Add drained corn, parsley, chili powder, garlic salt, cumin, ½ teaspoon *salt,* and ¼ teaspoon *pepper* to meat mixture; mix well. Stir in cream cheese and milk. Stir in macaroni; heat through.

Cut tomatoes into wedges. Arrange tomato wedges and cheese triangles atop meat mixture. Cover skillet and heat over low heat for 8 to 10 minutes or just till cheese is melted and tomatoes are heated through. Makes 4 or 5 servings.

To brown ground meat evenly, break up meat with the back of a spoon or a fork. Stir occasionally during cooking. Avoid breaking the meat into pieces that are too small.

Browning Meat in a Skillet

Saucy Beef and Cabbage Supper (pictured on page 80)

2 cups Frozen Beef Starter (see recipe, opposite)
1 medium head cabbage, cut into 6 wedges
2 tablespoons butter *or* margarine
2 tablespoons all-purpose flour
1 teaspoon instant beef bouillon granules
½ teaspoon celery seed
¼ teaspoon paprika
¼ teaspoon dried thyme, crushed
1¼ cups milk
½ cup shredded monterey jack cheese (2 ounces)
¼ cup dairy sour cream

To thaw Frozen Beef Starter, in saucepan combine frozen meat mixture and ¼ cup *water*. Cover and cook over low heat for 15 minutes; break up meat mixture with a fork. Cover and cook for 5 minutes longer. Drain off liquid.

In large covered skillet cook cabbage wedges in a small amount of boiling salted water about 10 minutes or just till tender. Drain cabbage well.

To make sauce, in medium saucepan melt butter or margarine. Stir in flour, beef bouillon granules, celery seed, paprika, thyme, and dash *pepper*. Add the milk all at once. Cook over medium heat, stirring constantly, till thickened and bubbly. Stir in monterey jack cheese and dairy sour cream. Heat through; *do not boil*. Stir in meat mixture.

Arrange drained cabbage wedges on serving plate. Pour some of the sauce over the cabbage wedges. Pass the remaining sauce. Makes 6 servings.

Quick and Easy Spaghetti Sauce

2 cups Frozen Beef Starter (see recipe, opposite)
1 15-ounce can tomato sauce
1 teaspoon dried oregano, crushed
1 teaspoon worcestershire sauce
½ teaspoon sugar
½ teaspoon dried basil, crushed
¼ teaspoon garlic powder
Hot cooked spaghetti

To thaw Frozen Beef Starter, in 2-quart saucepan combine frozen meat mixture and ¼ cup *water*. Cover and cook over low heat for 15 minutes; break up meat mixture with fork.

Stir in tomato sauce, oregano, worcestershire, sugar, basil, garlic powder, ¼ teaspoon *salt,* and ⅛ teaspoon *pepper*. Bring to boiling; reduce heat. Simmer, uncovered, about 15 minutes, stirring occasionally. Serve over hot spaghetti. If desired, pass grated parmesan cheese. Makes 4 servings.

Stir-Fried Beef with Vegetables

2 cups Frozen Beef Starter (see recipe, opposite)
1 teaspoon instant beef bouillon granules
2 tablespoons soy sauce
1 tablespoon cornstarch
2 tablespoons cooking oil
1 clove garlic, minced
1 teaspoon grated gingerroot
1 cup thinly sliced cauliflower
1 cup biased-sliced carrots
2 cups chopped bok choy *or* chopped spinach leaves
1 cup fresh pea pods *or* one 6-ounce package frozen pea pods, thawed
1 cup sliced fresh mushrooms
1 cup fresh bean sprouts *or* ½ of a 16-ounce can bean sprouts, drained
Hot cooked rice

To thaw Frozen Beef Starter, in saucepan combine frozen meat mixture and ¼ cup *water*. Cover and cook over low heat for 15 minutes; break up meat mixture with fork. Cover; cook 5 minutes longer. Set aside. In small bowl dissolve bouillon granules in ¾ cup boiling *water*. Combine soy sauce and cornstarch; stir in bouillon. Set aside.

Preheat large skillet or wok over high heat; add oil. Stir-fry garlic and gingerroot in hot oil for 30 seconds. Add cauliflower and carrots; stir-fry 3 minutes. Add bok choy or spinach, pea pods, mushrooms, and bean sprouts; stir-fry 2 minutes more or till vegetables are crisp-tender. Remove vegetables to bowl. (Add more oil to skillet or wok, if necessary.) Add meat mixture to hot skillet or wok; stir-fry 2 to 3 minutes or till meat is heated through. Push meat mixture from center of skillet or wok.

Stir beef bouillon mixture; add to center of skillet or wok. Cook and stir till bubbly. Return vegetables; stir together vegetables, bouillon mixture, and meat mixture. Cover; cook 1 minute. Serve at once with rice. Garnish with cherry tomato flower and green onion fan, if desired. Pass additional soy sauce, if desired. Makes 4 or 5 servings.

Saucy Beef and Cabbage Supper (see recipe, page 79), *Meat and Mac Skillet* (see recipe, page 78), and *Lamb Curry* with choice of condiments make appealing meals in a skillet.

Quick Cranberry Macaroni

1 pound ground beef
1 8-ounce can tomato sauce
1 8-ounce can jellied cranberry
   sauce
½ cup water
¼ cup bottled barbecue sauce
½ teaspoon salt
½ teaspoon ground ginger
¼ teaspoon ground cinnamon
   Hot cooked macaroni

In 10-inch skillet cook ground beef till browned. Drain off fat. Stir in tomato sauce, cranberry sauce, water, barbecue sauce, salt, ginger, and cinnamon. Cook, uncovered, over medium-low heat for 15 to 20 minutes, stirring occasionally. Serve over hot cooked macaroni. Makes 4 servings.

Sausage Stroganoff

1 pound bulk pork sausage,
   ground pork, *or* ground beef
1 cup chopped onion
1 cup sliced fresh mushrooms
1 clove garlic, minced
1 6-ounce can tomato paste
¾ cup water
½ cup dry red wine
2 tablespoons snipped parsley
1 teaspoon instant beef bouillon
   granules
½ teaspoon salt
½ teaspoon dried dillweed
   (optional)
   Dash pepper
1 cup dairy sour cream
1 tablespoon all-purpose flour
   Hot cooked noodles

In large skillet cook sausage, ground pork, or ground beef, onion, mushrooms, and garlic till meat is browned and vegetables are tender. Drain off fat. Stir tomato paste, water, red wine, snipped parsley, beef bouillon granules, salt, dillweed, and pepper into meat mixture. Bring to boiling; reduce heat. Cover and simmer for 10 minutes. Combine sour cream and flour; stir into meat mixture. Cook and stir till thickened; *do not boil*. Serve over hot cooked noodles. Makes 6 servings.

Lamb Curry

1 pound ground lamb *or* ground
   beef
1 cup chopped onion
1 clove garlic, minced
2 teaspoons curry powder
2 medium tomatoes, peeled and
   chopped
1 medium apple, peeled, cored,
   and chopped
½ cup water
1 teaspoon instant beef bouillon
   granules
¾ teaspoon salt
½ teaspoon ground ginger
¼ cup cold water
1 tablespoon all-purpose flour
   Parslied Rice
   Condiments (optional)

In 10-inch skillet cook ground lamb or ground beef, onion, and garlic till meat is browned and onion is tender. Drain off fat. Stir curry powder into meat mixture; cook 1 minute more. Stir in tomatoes, apple, the ½ cup water, beef bouillon granules, salt, and ginger. Cover and simmer for 5 to 10 minutes or till apple is tender.

Combine ¼ cup cold water and flour; stir into meat mixture. Cook and stir till thickened and bubbly. Serve over hot Parslied Rice. If desired, pass condiments such as raisins, shredded coconut, chopped cucumber, chutney, chopped peanuts, or crumbled crisp-cooked bacon. Makes 4 or 5 servings.

Parslied Rice: In a 2-quart saucepan combine 2 cups cold *water,* 1 cup long grain *rice,* 1 tablespoon *butter,* 2 teaspoons instant *chicken bouillon granules,* and ½ teaspoon *salt.* Cover with a tight-fitting lid. Bring to boiling; turn heat to low. Continue cooking for 15 minutes (do not lift cover). Remove from heat and let stand, covered, for 10 minutes. Stir in ¼ cup snipped *parsley.*

Ground Beef Oriental

1   9-ounce package frozen
    French-style green beans
¾   pound ground beef
½   cup chopped onion
¼   cup soy sauce
2   tablespoons water
⅛   teaspoon garlic powder
⅛   teaspoon pepper
2   cups cooked rice
2   tablespoons butter *or*
    margarine
2   slightly beaten eggs
1   cup fresh bean sprouts

Rinse green beans under hot water to separate. Set aside. In a preheated large skillet or wok stir-fry ground beef and onion, leaving meat in large chunks, till meat is browned and onion is tender. Drain off fat. Stir soy sauce, water, garlic powder, and pepper into meat mixture. Remove from pan; keep warm. Add green beans to skillet; cook 2 to 3 minutes. Stir in rice; push mixture to sides of skillet. Melt butter or margarine in center of skillet; add eggs and stir-fry just till set. Carefully stir rice and meat mixtures into egg mixture. Stir in sprouts, cook 1 to 2 minutes. Makes 4 servings.

Pork Chop Suey

1   pound ground pork *or* ground
    beef
1   cup sliced onion
2   cups fresh bean sprouts *or*
    one 16-ounce can bean
    sprouts, drained
2   cups sliced fresh mushrooms
1   cup bias-sliced celery
½   of an 8-ounce can water
    chestnuts, drained and
    thinly sliced
⅓   cup chopped green pepper
1   16-ounce can chop suey
    vegetables, drained
1   10½-ounce can condensed beef
    broth
⅓   cup soy sauce
⅓   cup cold water
2   tablespoons cornstarch
    Hot cooked rice
    Chow mein noodles

In 12-inch skillet cook ground pork or ground beef and onion till meat is browned and onion is tender. Drain off fat. Stir in bean sprouts, mushrooms, celery, water chestnuts, and green pepper. Cook and stir 2 minutes. Stir in chop suey vegetables, beef broth, and soy sauce. Bring to boiling; cover and cook over low heat for 2 to 3 minutes.

Combine cold water and cornstarch; stir into vegetable mixture. Cook over medium heat, stirring constantly, till mixture is thickened and bubbly. Serve over hot cooked rice; sprinkle with chow mein noodles. Pass additional soy sauce, if desired. Makes 6 servings.

Texas Beef Skillet

1   pound ground beef
¾   cup chopped onion
1   16-ounce can tomatoes, cut up
1   15½-ounce can red kidney beans
½   cup quick-cooking rice
½   cup water
3   tablespoons chopped green
    pepper
1½ teaspoons chili powder
½   teaspoon salt
½   teaspoon garlic salt
¾   cup shredded American cheese
    Corn chips, crushed

In skillet cook ground beef and onion till meat is browned and onion is tender. Drain off fat. Stir in *undrained* tomatoes, *undrained* beans, rice, water, green pepper, chili powder, salt, and garlic salt. Bring to boiling; reduce heat. Cover and simmer for 20 minutes, stirring occasionally. Top meat mixture with shredded cheese. Cover and heat about 3 minutes or till cheese melts. Sprinkle corn chips around edge. Makes 6 servings.

Sausage-Noodle Skillet

1 pound bulk pork sausage
1 16-ounce can tomatoes, cut up
1 15½-ounce can red kidney
    beans, drained
1½ cups water
1 8-ounce can tomato sauce
½ cup chopped green pepper
2 teaspoons minced dried onion
1 to 2 teaspoons chili powder
4 ounces medium noodles (3 cups)

In skillet cook sausage till meat is browned. Drain off fat. Stir in *undrained* tomatoes, red kidney beans, water, tomato sauce, green pepper, dried onion, chili powder, and ½ teaspoon *salt*. Stir in *uncooked* noodles. Bring to boiling; reduce heat. Simmer, uncovered, for 25 to 30 minutes or till noodles are tender. Makes 4 or 5 servings.

Spanish Rice Skillet

1 pound ground beef
3 slices bacon, chopped
½ cup chopped onion
¼ cup chopped green pepper
1 16-ounce can tomatoes, cut up
2 cups water
1 cup long grain rice
½ cup chili sauce
1 teaspoon worcestershire sauce

In skillet cook ground beef, bacon, onion, and green pepper till meat is browned and vegetables are tender. Drain off fat. Stir in *undrained* tomatoes, water, *uncooked* rice, chili sauce, worcestershire sauce, 1 teaspoon *salt,* and ⅛ teaspoon *pepper.* Bring to boiling; reduce heat. Cover and simmer for 25 to 30 minutes or till liquid is absorbed and rice is tender. Makes 6 servings.

Skillet Enchiladas

1 10¾-ounce can condensed
    cream of mushroom soup
1 10-ounce can enchilada sauce
¼ cup milk
2 tablespoons chopped canned
    green chili peppers
8 canned tortillas *or* frozen
    tortillas, thawed
    Cooking oil (optional)
2½ cups shredded American
    cheese (10 ounces)
½ cup chopped pitted ripe olives
1 pound ground beef
½ cup chopped onion

To make hot sauce, in saucepan combine mushroom soup, enchilada sauce, milk, and green chili peppers; heat till bubbly. Dip tortillas, one at a time, in hot sauce just till tortillas become limp. (Or, heat some cooking oil in a small skillet; dip tortillas in oil till limp.) Drain tortillas. Set aside ½ cup cheese. Place ¼ *cup* of the cheese on *each* tortilla; sprinkle with olives. Roll up jelly-roll style.

In skillet cook ground beef and onion till meat is browned and onion is tender; drain off fat. Stir in hot sauce. Arrange tortillas, seam side down, in meat mixture in the skillet. Bring to boiling; reduce heat. Cover and cook about 5 minutes or till heated through. Sprinkle with the reserved ½ cup cheese; cover and cook about 1 minute longer or till cheese melts. Makes 6 to 8 servings.

Microwave cooking directions: To make hot sauce, in 12x7½x2-inch nonmetal baking dish combine mushroom soup, enchilada sauce, milk, and green chili peppers. Cook, uncovered, in countertop microwave oven on high power about 5 minutes or till bubbly, stirring sauce 3 times. Dip tortillas in hot sauce or cooking oil as directed above. Fill and roll up as directed above.

In nonmetal bowl crumble ground beef; add onion. Micro-cook, covered with waxed paper, about 5 minutes or till meat is done, stirring several times. Drain off fat. Stir meat into hot sauce in baking dish.

Arrange tortillas, seam side down, in meat mixture. Micro-cook, uncovered, about 8 minutes, or till hot, giving dish a quarter turn every 3 minutes. Sprinkle with ½ cup cheese.

Sweet-Sour Beef 'n' Cabbage

1½ pounds ground beef
½ cup chopped onion
½ cup sliced celery
½ cup chopped green pepper
2 tablespoons quick-cooking
   rolled oats
2 tablespoons snipped parsley
¾ teaspoon salt
¼ teaspoon garlic powder
⅛ teaspoon pepper
1 medium head cabbage
1 15-ounce can tomato sauce
¼ cup cider vinegar
3 tablespoons brown sugar
½ teaspoon salt
   Dash pepper

In skillet cook ground beef, onion, celery, and green pepper till meat is browned; drain off fat. Sprinkle meat mixture with rolled oats, parsley, the ¾ teaspoon salt, garlic powder, and the ⅛ teaspoon pepper.

Core cabbage; cut into six wedges. Place atop meat. In bowl combine tomato sauce, vinegar, brown sugar, the ½ teaspoon salt, and the dash pepper; mix well. Pour over cabbage and meat. Cover and simmer for 15 to 20 minutes or till cabbage is tender. Serve at once. Makes 6 servings.

Ham and Cabbage Rolls

1 cup water
⅓ cup long grain rice
2 teaspoons instant chicken
   bouillon granules
2 beaten eggs
¼ cup finely chopped onion
¼ cup finely chopped green
   pepper
¼ teaspoon salt
¼ teaspoon dried thyme, crushed
¼ teaspoon dried savory, crushed
   Dash pepper
3 cups ground fully cooked ham
12 large cabbage leaves
1 cup dairy sour cream
2 tablespoons all-purpose flour

In saucepan bring water, rice, and *1 teaspoon* of the chicken bouillon granules to boiling. Reduce heat; cover and simmer about 20 minutes or till tender. Combine cooked rice, eggs, onion, green pepper, salt, thyme, savory, and pepper. Add ground ham; mix well.

Immerse cabbage leaves in boiling water about 3 minutes or just till limp; drain. Cut about 2 inches of heavy center vein out of each cabbage leaf. Place about ¼ cup meat mixture in center of *each* leaf; fold in sides. Fold ends to overlap atop meat mixture. Place, seam side down, in 10-inch skillet. Dissolve the remaining 1 teaspoon bouillon granules in 1 cup hot *water;* pour over cabbage rolls. Cover and simmer about 25 minutes or till tender. Remove cabbage rolls to warm platter; keep warm. Combine sour cream and flour; stir into pan juices. Cook and stir till thickened and bubbly. Spoon over cabbage rolls. Makes 6 servings.

Fettuccine with Sausage and Peppers

1 pound bulk pork sausage *or*
   bulk Italian sausage
2 medium sweet red *or* green
   peppers, coarsely chopped
1 cup chopped onion
1 clove garlic, minced
1 cup light cream
¼ cup snipped parsley
1 teaspoon dried marjoram,
   crushed
½ teaspoon salt
⅛ teaspoon pepper
10 ounces fettuccine *or* spaghetti
½ cup grated parmesan cheese

In large skillet cook sausage, red or green peppers, onion, and garlic till meat is browned and vegetables are tender. Drain off fat. Stir in cream, parsley, marjoram, salt, and pepper. Bring to boiling; reduce heat. Cook and stir over medium heat for 6 to 8 minutes or till slightly thickened.

Meanwhile, cook fettuccine or spaghetti in a large amount of boiling salted water for 10 to 12 minutes or just till tender; drain. Toss sausage mixture and parmesan cheese with cooked fettuccine or spaghetti till coated. Serve immediately. Makes 4 servings.

Turn to *Sweet-Sour Beef 'n' Cabbage* for an easy, one-dish meal. The cooked
cabbage tends to water out (and thin the sauce), so it is best served as soon as it is ready.

Spaghetti Sauce

1½ pounds ground beef *or* bulk
      pork sausage
1 large onion, chopped
1 large green pepper, chopped
2 cloves garlic, minced
3 16-ounce cans tomatoes, cut up
1 6-ounce can tomato paste
2 teaspoons brown sugar
1½ teaspoons dried oregano,
      crushed
½ teaspoon dried basil, crushed
½ teaspoon dried thyme, crushed
1 bay leaf
  Hot cooked spaghetti

In Dutch oven cook ground beef or sausage, onion, green pepper, and garlic till meat is browned and vegetables are tender. Drain off fat. Stir in *undrained* tomatoes, tomato paste, brown sugar, oregano, basil, thyme, bay leaf, 2 cups *water,* and 1 teaspoon *salt.* Bring to boiling; reduce heat. Simmer, uncovered, for 1½ to 2 hours or till desired consistency, stirring occasionally. Remove bay leaf. Serve with spaghetti. Pass grated parmesan cheese, if desired. Makes 6 servings.

Olive Spaghetti Sauce (pictured on pages 76 and 77)

1 pound ground beef
½ pound bulk Italian sausage
1 28-ounce can tomatoes, cut up
2 6-ounce cans tomato paste
1½ cups burgundy
1 cup chopped onion
¾ cup chopped green pepper
3 bay leaves
2 cloves garlic, minced
1½ teaspoons worcestershire sauce
1 teaspoon sugar
½ teaspoon chili powder
1 6-ounce can sliced mushrooms
½ cup sliced pimiento-stuffed
      olives
  Hot cooked spaghetti

In Dutch oven cook ground beef and sausage till browned; drain off fat. Stir in *undrained* tomatoes, tomato paste, burgundy, onion, green pepper, bay leaves, garlic, worcestershire, sugar, chili powder, 1 cup *water,* 1 teaspoon *salt,* and ⅛ teaspoon *pepper.* Simmer, uncovered, for 2 hours, stirring occasionally. Remove bay leaves. Stir in *undrained* mushrooms and olives; simmer about 30 minutes longer. Serve with spaghetti. Pass grated parmesan cheese, if desired. Makes 8 servings.

Northern Italian Meat Sauce

3 slices bacon, cut up
1 pound ground beef
½ pound ground veal *or* ground
      pork*
1 28-ounce can tomatoes, cut up
2 *or* 3 chicken livers, chopped
      (optional)
1 cup chopped onion
¼ cup finely chopped carrot
¼ cup finely chopped celery
¼ cup snipped parsley
¼ cup tomato paste
½ teaspoon instant chicken
      bouillon granules
⅛ teaspoon ground nutmeg
½ cup dry white wine
  Hot cooked spaghetti

In large saucepan or Dutch oven cook bacon till crisp. Add ground beef and ground veal or ground pork*; cook till meat is browned. Drain off fat.

If desired, press *undrained* tomatoes through food mill or sieve. Add *undrained* tomatoes, chicken livers, onion, carrot, celery, parsley, tomato paste, bouillon granules, nutmeg, 1 teaspoon *salt,* and ¼ teaspoon *pepper* to meat mixture. Stir in wine and ¼ cup *water.* Bring to boiling; reduce heat. Boil gently, uncovered, for 45 to 60 minutes or till desired consistency, stirring occasionally.

Just before serving, stir ⅓ cup light *cream or milk* into the hot sauce, if desired. Serve with spaghetti. Pass grated parmesan cheese, if desired. Makes 6 servings.

Note: Or, substitute an additional ½ pound ground *beef* for the ground veal or ground pork.

Skillet Pizza

1 15⅜-ounce package cheese
    pizza mix
½ cup hot water
1 tablespoon Italian seasoning
    or dried basil, crushed
½ pound bulk pork sausage *or*
    bulk Italian sausage
½ cup sliced pitted ripe olives
1½ cups shredded mozzarella
    cheese (6 ounces)

In bowl combine flour packet from pizza mix and hot water to form a soft dough. With greased hands spread dough into a greased cold heavy 10-inch skillet. Press over bottom and ½ inch up sides. Cook over medium-low heat for 7 minutes with lid of skillet ajar. Meanwhile, combine sauce from mix and Italian seasoning or basil. In another skillet brown sausage; drain off fat. Stir in *half* of the sauce mixture.

Spread remaining sauce mixture over crust; sprinkle with cheese from mix. Top with sausage mixture and olives. Sprinkle with mozzarella. Cook over medium-low heat for 15 minutes with lid ajar. Uncover; cook 6 to 8 minutes. Loosen sides and bottom of pizza; slide onto plate. Makes 4 servings.

Chicken Croquettes

3 tablespoons butter *or*
    margarine
¼ cup all-purpose flour
½ teaspoon instant chicken
    bouillon granules
⅓ cup milk
1 tablespoon finely chopped
    onion
1 tablespoon snipped parsley
1 teaspoon lemon juice
    Dash ground nutmeg
    Dash paprika
1½ cups coarsely ground *cooked*
    chicken *or* turkey
¾ cup fine dry bread crumbs *or*
    finely crushed saltine
    crackers
1 beaten egg
    Shortening *or* cooking oil for
    deep-fat frying

In saucepan melt butter or margarine; stir in flour and bouillon granules. Add milk and ½ cup *water* all at once; cook and stir till thickened and bubbly. Cook and stir 1 minute more. Remove from heat. Stir in onion, parsley, lemon juice, nutmeg, paprika, ¼ teaspoon *salt,* and dash *pepper.* Add ground cooked chicken or turkey; mix well. Cover and chill thoroughly.

With wet hands shape chicken mixture into 8 balls. Roll in bread or cracker crumbs; shape each ball into a cone. In shallow dish combine beaten egg and 2 tablespoons *water.* Dip each croquette into egg mixture; roll again in crumbs. Fry, a few at a time, in deep hot fat (365°) for 2½ to 3 minutes or till golden brown. Drain on paper toweling. Keep warm in 325° oven while frying remaining croquettes. Makes 4 servings.

Chicken-Ham Croquettes: Prepare Chicken Croquettes as above *except* use 1 cup coarsely ground *cooked chicken or turkey* and ½ cup coarsely ground fully cooked *ham* for the meat mixture and omit the salt.

Ham Croquettes with Cheese Sauce (pictured on pages 76 and 77)

3 tablespoons butter *or*
    margarine
¼ to ½ teaspoon curry powder
¼ cup all-purpose flour
¾ cup milk
2 teaspoons prepared mustard
1 teaspoon grated onion
2 cups coarsely ground fully
    cooked ham
⅔ cup fine dry bread crumbs
1 beaten egg
2 tablespoons water
    Shortening *or* cooking oil for
    deep-fat frying
    Cheese Sauce

Melt butter or margarine with curry powder; stir in flour. Add milk all at once; cook and stir till bubbly. Cook and stir 2 minutes more. Remove from heat. Stir in mustard and onion. Add ground ham; mix well. Cover and chill thoroughly. With wet hands shape mixture into 10 balls. Roll in bread crumbs; shape each ball into a cone. Dip into mixture of egg and water; roll again in crumbs. Fry, a few at a time, in deep hot fat (365°) for 2 to 2½ minutes or till golden brown. Drain; keep warm. Serve with Cheese Sauce. Makes 5 servings.

Cheese Sauce: In saucepan melt 2 tablespoons *butter or margarine.* Stir in 2 tablespoons all-purpose *flour,* ¼ teaspoon *salt,* and dash *pepper.* Add 1¼ cups *milk* all at once. Cook and stir till thickened and bubbly. Cook and stir 2 minutes more. Add ½ cup shredded *American cheese* and ½ cup shredded *Swiss cheese;* heat and stir till melted.

South of the Border Salad (pictured on pages 76 and 77)

1 pound bulk pork sausage *or* ground beef
½ cup chopped onion
1 clove garlic, minced
1 8-ounce can tomato sauce
1 7½-ounce can tomatoes, cut up
1 4-ounce can green chili peppers, rinsed, seeded, and finely chopped
1 tablespoon all-purpose flour
2 teaspoons chili powder
6 cups torn lettuce
1 15-ounce can garbanzo beans, drained
½ cup sliced pitted ripe olives
1 cup shredded monterey jack *or* cheddar cheese (4 ounces)
1 cup cherry tomatoes, halved
1 green pepper, cut into strips
1 avocado

In skillet cook sausage or ground beef, onion, and garlic till meat is browned and onion is tender. Drain off fat. Stir in tomato sauce, *undrained* tomatoes, chili peppers, flour, and chili powder. Cook and stir till thickened and bubbly.

Meanwhile, in salad bowl combine lettuce, garbanzo beans, and olives; toss. Top with meat mixture; sprinkle with shredded cheese. Top with cherry tomato halves and green pepper strips. Peel and slice avocado; arrange slices atop salad. If desired, sprinkle with ½ cup shelled *pumpkin seed,* toasted. Makes 6 servings.

Note: If you prefer, toss lettuce, garbanzo beans, and olives and divide mixture among six individual salad plates. Top each salad with some of the remaining ingredients.

Ham Mousse

1 envelope unflavored gelatin
1 beaten egg
1½ teaspoons instant chicken bouillon granules
¼ cup mayonnaise
1 tablespoon chopped green onion
2 teaspoons dijon-style mustard
1½ cups ground fully cooked ham
½ cup whipping cream

Soften gelatin in ½ cup *cold water;* set aside. Combine beaten egg, bouillon granules, and ⅔ cup *water.* Cook and stir over low heat about 7 minutes or till slightly thickened. Add softened gelatin; stir till dissolved. Beat in mayonnaise, green onion, and mustard. Stir in ground ham. Chill till partially set. Whip cream to soft peaks; fold into ham mixture. Turn mixture into 5 or 6 individual molds. Chill till set. Unmold; serve on lettuce-lined plates, if desired. Makes 5 or 6 servings.

Egg Rolls

¾ pound ground pork
1 clove garlic, minced
1 tablespoon cooking oil
2 cups finely chopped bok choy
1 cup finely chopped fresh mushrooms
½ cup thinly sliced green onion
½ cup finely chopped water chestnuts
½ cup finely shredded carrot
2 tablespoons soy sauce
2 teaspoons cornstarch
½ teaspoon sugar
¼ teaspoon salt
12 egg roll skins
Shortening *or* cooking oil for deep-fat frying
Sweet and Sour Sauce

In skillet stir-fry pork and garlic in 1 tablespoon hot oil till meat is browned. Drain off fat. Add vegetables; stir-fry 2 to 3 minutes. Mix soy sauce, cornstarch, sugar, and salt. Stir into pork mixture; cook and stir till thickened. Cool.

To wrap egg rolls, place egg roll skin with one point toward you. Spoon about ¼ cup pork mixture horizontally across and just below center of skin. Fold bottom point of skin over filling; tuck point under filling. Fold in sides. Roll up toward remaining corner; moisten point and press firmly to seal. Fry egg rolls, a few at a time, in deep hot fat (365°) for 2 to 3 minutes or till golden. Drain. Serve with Sweet and Sour Sauce. Makes 12.

Sweet and Sour Sauce: Combine ½ cup packed *brown sugar* and 1 tablespoon *cornstarch.* Stir in ⅓ cup *red wine vinegar,* ⅓ cup *water,* ¼ cup finely chopped *green pepper,* 2 tablespoons chopped *pimiento,* 1 tablespoon *soy sauce,* ¼ teaspoon instant *chicken bouillon granules,* ¼ teaspoon ground *ginger,* and ¼ teaspoon *garlic powder.* Cook and stir till bubbly.

French Omelet

3 eggs
1 tablespoon water
¼ teaspoon salt
  Dash pepper
1 tablespoon butter *or* margarine
  Oriental Beef filling *or* Pork
    and Mushroom filling (see
    recipes, below)

In a small bowl beat together eggs, water, salt, and pepper with a fork till mixture is blended but not frothy. In an 8-inch skillet with flared sides, heat butter or margarine over medium heat till butter sizzles and browns slightly. Lift and tilt pan to coat the sides.

Add egg mixture; cook over medium heat. As eggs set, run a spatula around edge of skillet, lifting the eggs to allow uncooked portion to flow underneath. When eggs are set but still shiny, remove from heat. Spoon desired filling across the center. Using a metal spatula, carefully lift one-third of omelet and fold over center; overlap the remaining third of omelet over center. Slide omelet to edge of skillet. Tilt skillet and slide omelet out onto serving plate. (*Or,* fill omelet. Fold omelet in half; tilt pan and slide omelet out onto serving plate.) Serve immediately. Makes 2 servings.

Oriental Beef Omelets (pictured on page 91)

½ pound ground beef *or* ground
    pork
½ cup cold water
2 tablespoons soy sauce
1 tablespoon cornstarch
¼ teaspoon ground ginger
¼ teaspoon garlic powder
2 cups small spinach leaves
½ of a 16-ounce can bean
    sprouts, drained
½ cup thinly sliced bamboo
    shoots
3 French Omelets (see recipe,
    above)

In skillet cook ground beef or ground pork till meat is browned; drain off fat. Combine cold water, soy sauce, cornstarch, ginger, and garlic powder; stir into meat. Cook and stir till thickened and bubbly. Stir in spinach leaves, bean sprouts, and bamboo shoots. Cover and cook over low heat about 5 minutes or till heated through. Keep warm.

Prepare one French Omelet at a time, filling *each* omelet with *one-third* of the meat mixture. Keep warm in a 325° oven while preparing the remaining omelets. Makes 6 servings.

Pork and Mushroom Omelets (pictured on page 91)

½ pound ground pork *or* bulk pork
    sausage
1 cup sliced fresh mushrooms
½ cup chopped onion
1 clove garlic, minced
½ cup dairy sour cream
2 tablespoons snipped parsley
1 tablespoon milk
½ teaspoon salt
½ teaspoon dry mustard
3 French Omelets (see recipe,
    above)
  Shredded cheddar, Swiss, *or*
    monterey jack cheese
    (optional)

In medium skillet cook ground pork or sausage, mushrooms, onion, and garlic till meat is browned and onion is tender. Drain off fat. Reduce heat. Stir in sour cream, parsley, milk, salt, and dry mustard. Heat through; *do not boil.* Keep warm.

Prepare one French Omelet at a time, filling *each* omelet with *one-third* of the meat mixture. Keep warm in a 325° oven while preparing the remaining omelets. Sprinkle omelets with shredded cheese, if desired. Makes 6 servings.

Meat Frittata

½ **pound ground beef** *or* **bulk pork sausage**
¼ **cup chopped onion**
¼ **cup chopped green pepper**
6 **beaten eggs**
⅓ **cup milk**
½ **teaspoon dried oregano, crushed**
⅛ **teaspoon pepper**
2 **tablespoons olive oil, cooking oil, butter,** *or* **margarine**
 Grated parmesan *or* **romano cheese**
 Snipped parsley

In skillet cook ground beef or sausage, onion, and green pepper till meat is browned and vegetables are tender. Drain off fat. If using ground beef, season the meat with ½ teaspoon *salt*. In mixing bowl combine eggs, milk, oregano, pepper, and ½ teaspoon *salt*. Stir in meat mixture.

In a 10-inch oven-going skillet, heat the oil, butter, or margarine over medium-low heat. Pour egg mixture into skillet. As eggs set, run a spatula around edge of skillet, lifting egg mixture to allow uncooked portion to flow underneath. Continue cooking and lifting edges till mixture is almost set (surface will be moist). The total cooking time should be about 6 minutes.

Place skillet under the broiler 5 inches from heat. Broil about 1 minute or just till top is set. Sprinkle with parmesan or romano cheese and snipped parsley. Loosen bottom of frittata and slide out onto a serving plate. Cut frittata into wedges. Makes 4 servings.

Crepe-Style Manicotti

16 **Main Dish Crepes (see recipe, below)**
½ **pound ground beef** *or* **ground pork**
½ **cup chopped onion**
1 **small clove garlic, minced**
1 **7½-ounce can tomatoes, cut up**
1 **6-ounce can tomato paste**
½ **cup water**
1½ **teaspoons dried basil, crushed**
¾ **teaspoon salt**
½ **teaspoon sugar**
¼ **teaspoon fennel seed, crushed**
2 **beaten eggs**
3 **cups ricotta** *or* **cream-style cottage cheese**
¼ **cup grated parmesan cheese**
1 **tablespoon dried parsley flakes**
½ **teaspoon salt**
¼ **teaspoon pepper**
1 **cup shredded mozzarella cheese (4 ounces)**

Prepare Main Dish Crepes; set aside. In skillet cook ground beef or ground pork, onion, and garlic till meat is browned and onion is tender. Drain off fat. Stir in *undrained* tomatoes, tomato paste, water, basil, ¾ teaspoon salt, sugar, and fennel seed. Cover and simmer for 15 minutes, stirring frequently. For filling combine beaten eggs, ricotta or cottage cheese, parmesan cheese, parsley, ½ teaspoon salt, and pepper.

Spread about *3 tablespoons* filling over unbrowned side of *each* crepe. Roll up jelly-roll style. Place, seam side down, in 13x9x2-inch baking dish. Spoon meat mixture over crepes. Cover and bake in 375° oven for 25 minutes. Uncover; sprinkle with shredded mozzarella cheese. Bake till cheese is melted. Makes 8 servings.

Main Dish Crepes

1 **cup all-purpose flour**
1½ **cups milk**
2 **eggs**
1 **tablespoon cooking oil**
¼ **teaspoon salt**

In bowl combine flour, milk, eggs, oil, and salt; beat with a rotary beater till blended. Heat a lightly greased 6-inch skillet; remove from heat. Spoon in about *2 tablespoons* batter; lift and tilt skillet to spread batter evenly. Return to heat; brown on one side only. Invert pan over paper toweling; remove crepe. Repeat with remaining batter to make 16 to 18 crepes, greasing skillet as needed.

Delicate omelets and feather-light crepes form the beginnings of *Oriental Beef Omelets* folded in half, *Pork and Mushroom Omelets* (see recipes, page 89), and *Crepe-Style Manicotti.*

Sweet-Sour Burger Crepes

12 **Main Dish Crepes (see recipe, page 90)**
 1 **15½-ounce can pineapple chunks**
 ⅓ **cup packed brown sugar**
 2 **tablespoons cornstarch**
 ¼ **teaspoon salt**
 ⅛ **teaspoon ground ginger**
 ⅓ **cup vinegar**
 1 **tablespoon soy sauce**
 1 **medium green pepper, cut into ½-inch cubes**
 ¾ **pound ground beef**
 ½ **cup chopped onion**
 ½ **teaspoon salt**
 ⅛ **teaspoon pepper**

Prepare Main Dish Crepes; set aside. For sauce drain pineapple, reserving syrup. Add enough water to syrup to make 1 cup liquid. In saucepan combine brown sugar, cornstarch, ¼ teaspoon salt, and ginger. Stir in reserved 1 cup pineapple liquid; add vinegar and soy sauce. Cook and stir till thickened and bubbly. Reserve ⅓ *cup* of the sauce. Stir pineapple and green pepper into remaining sauce; set aside.

In skillet cook ground beef and onion till meat is browned and onion is tender. Drain off fat. Stir in the reserved ⅓ cup sauce, ½ teaspoon salt, and pepper.

Spoon about 3 *tablespoons* meat mixture along center of unbrowned side of *each* crepe. Fold two opposite edges so they overlap atop meat mixture. Place, seam side down, in 13x9x2-inch baking dish. Cover; bake in 375° oven about 20 minutes. Reheat pineapple-green pepper sauce; spoon over crepes. Makes 6 servings.

Home-Style Pork Pie Crepes

12 **Main Dish Crepes (see recipe, page 90)**
 1 **pound ground pork**
 ¾ **cup water**
 ½ **cup finely chopped onion**
 ¼ **cup fine dry bread crumbs**
 1 **teaspoon salt**
 ⅛ **teaspoon ground sage**
   Dash pepper
 2 **tablespoons butter *or* margarine**
 2 **tablespoons all-purpose flour**
 2 **cups milk**

Prepare Main Dish Crepes; set aside. In skillet cook ground pork till meat is browned; drain off fat. Stir in water, onion, bread crumbs, salt, sage, and pepper. Cover and simmer for 20 minutes. Spread about ¼ *cup* meat mixture over unbrowned side of *each* crepe, leaving ¼-inch rim around edge. Roll up jelly-roll style. Place, seam side down, in 13x9x2-inch baking dish. Cover and bake in 375° oven about 20 minutes or till heated through.

Meanwhile, for sauce melt butter or margarine. Stir in flour, 1 teaspoon *salt,* and dash *pepper;* add milk. Cook and stir till thickened and bubbly; cook and stir 2 minutes more. Spoon sauce over crepes. Sprinkle with snipped parsley and ground nutmeg, if desired. Makes 6 servings.

Sausage-Filled Crepes

12 **Main Dish Crepes (see recipe, page 90)**
 1 **pound bulk pork sausage *or* ground pork**
 ¼ **cup chopped onion**
 2 **cups sliced fresh mushrooms**
 ¾ **cup dairy sour cream**
 ½ **cup shredded American cheese**
 1 **3-ounce package cream cheese, softened**
 1 **tablespoon milk**
 ¼ **teaspoon celery salt *or* garlic salt**
 ¼ **teaspoon paprika**
 ¼ **teaspoon dried marjoram, crushed**
 ¼ **cup butter, softened**
 ¼ **cup dairy sour cream**

Prepare Main Dish Crepes; set aside. In saucepan cook sausage or ground pork and onion till meat is browned and onion is tender. Stir in mushrooms; cook for 1 minute. Drain off fat. Combine ¾ cup sour cream, American cheese, cream cheese, milk, celery salt or garlic salt, paprika, and marjoram. Stir into meat mixture. In small bowl stir together butter and the remaining ¼ cup sour cream.

Spoon about ¼ *cup* meat mixture over unbrowned side of *each* crepe, leaving ¼-inch rim around edge. Fold two opposite edges so they overlap atop meat mixture. Place, seam side down, in 12x7½x2-inch baking dish. Spread butter-sour cream mixture over crepes. Cover and bake in 375° oven about 25 minutes or till heated through. Sprinkle with snipped parsley, if desired. Makes 6 servings.

Index

T-Z

Tips